The Girl

A Mother's Memoir to Her Daughter

By

W J KENDRICK

ISBN: 1470198940
ISBN 13: 9781470198947

"Dedicated to my beloved mother and gorgeous daugher"

Table of Contents

Introduction

"When I first dreamed of having a little girl,
I was a child myself…"

And so this is where my journey ends: a beautiful baby girl named Angelica prepares to finish her undergraduate college degree and considers graduate school. The end has always been my desire. However, the journey was turbulent at times and pushed us down separate paths, miles away from both our desired destinations.

When I first dreamed of having a little girl, I was a child myself—a mixed-race girl who enjoyed the seemingly endless days of almost-warm British summers nestled in the hills of Northern London. St Paul's Cathedral and the London skyline served as a backdrop and made my maturing imagination even more vibrant. I spent most of my summer holidays in a large, abandoned construction site opposite our Tudor-style flats. The place was full of curious wonders of nature mixed with dilapidated building materials. I would sit on a piece of cement block or a large, appropriately positioned rock. Soon I would be imagining my future into existence with the help of a friend who had similar grandiose visions, or by myself, my glorious thoughts unrestricted by life's adult boundaries.

Predictably, my dreams ended with a beautiful baby girl. Curiously, I never imagined her looking like me. Instead, I always pictured a beautiful piece of perfection dressed in a pink, frilly dress similar to the one I wore in my first official portrait. And that's where my imagination ended and my story began.

Chapter One

"Reality distorted the images of my perfect labor."

A Dream Come True: My Baby Girl

It was the kind of pain that was both exhilarating and exhausting all in the same breath. The kind of pain that makes you feel strong and powerful at the beginning, faint and fragile at the end. I was having my first real childbirth contraction.

This is almost where my memories begin. I lay in the back of the car with a pillow under my head; I felt a mixture of uncertainty and excitement. My first child was due in four days but preferred a birth date of January 27 to the doctor's date of February 1. I felt as if I were living apart from the moment. I could hear Aaron, my cute US Marine husband, in the distance, requesting me to tell him when I had a contraction. *A contraction? What's a contraction?* I kept asking myself. I just felt pain, lots of pain. Suddenly the car jerked and went around in endless circles. All I could see was a series of trees blurred against the blue winter sky. I watched the blur and waited for my next contraction. I wondered whether the never-ending circle of trees also needed me to declare my contraction history before we could continue.

Looking back, I obviously was not thinking correctly. However, in that moment my thoughts were the clearest on earth. Why was my husband acting so strange and detached? We made what was hopefully the last circle. Aaron had talked on the phone to his mother before we left the house, something about picking up his older brother. The car made a final U-turn, presumably to pick up my brother-in-law. My husband and brother-in-law's faces, particularly the distinct twinkles in their eyes and the similar ways their faces burst into smiles, clearly identified them as brothers. However, in so many ways their differences were startling, at least to me an only child who expected siblings to act and look practically like replicas of the initial model.

Once my brother-in-law was safely seated in the passenger seat, we were off again, speeding down the road. Aaron no longer asked about contractions. I didn't particularly want to discuss the frequency anyway; the contraction pain was continuous and unrelenting. I could hear my experienced brother-in-law telling Aaron to slow down because we had plenty of time. He had an eighteen-month-old, and his wife had been in the hospital for a day before they gave birth. Fatherly instinct told Aaron differently. It wasn't long before we reached the hospital.

Reality distorted the images of my perfect labor. I had imagined Aaron and me in a birthing room, comfortable with each other. I envisioned us spending hours talking about the future, waiting, anticipating. We would discuss our hopes and dreams for our daughter. Our shared desires would correct any inadequacy in our own upbringings as we nurtured Angelica. What college should she attend? What professions should we consider? Initially only the occasional contraction would disturb our precious time together. As the contractions started to intrude on our special time, I envisioned an epidural wiping out the pain as science took over.

Instead, my husband dropped me off at the hospital entrance. My brother-in-law wheeled me in on a wheelchair. Ouch, the pain was nearly unbearable. The nurses had been expecting me for a quick checkup. Aaron had called the doctor's office earlier. His details about the length of my contractions were vague at best. The doctor's staff was convinced I was in premature labor. This was my first child, so there had been a good chance I would deliver late. However, my doctor was already at the hospital, so they recommended I come in for a quick check. When the labor and delivery nurse saw me doubled over in the wheelchair, unable to talk, she knew I was about to have a baby. "No birthing room, no epidural for her," I heard her mumble under her breath.

The next few minutes were a whirlwind of mandatory paperwork. My mind focused on certain unnecessary activities such as taking my clothes off. My subconscious protested: *Who cares about removing clothes? Surely just the removal of my pants is necessary.* Futile activities included the endless form-filling of official papers I was expected to read and sign between never-ending contractions. *Forms! I am going through torture. Who cares about signing forms? Is it legal to have me sign forms now?* Aaron appeared in the little closet that had been made into an examining room. I recall someone saying, "She's nine centimeters. Call the doctor. We are about to have a baby." A nurse to the side asked Aaron if he was all right. *Had he fainted?* I thought.

They instructed Aaron in a litany of next-step procedures. He disappeared again. *Why are they sending him away? That's not how it's supposed to happen!* was all my little inner voice could utter.

The next thing I knew, I was in the operating theater. I was not sure how I'd gotten there although I was sure I had not walked. The doctor arrived and mumbled something about knowing the difference between different types of contractions and practicing my breathing techniques. *What breathing techniques?* I thought. I searched my brain for classes on breathing the doctor insisted I had taken. But no memory was returned. *What breathing techniques?* I thought again. Aaron returned just in time. I was no longer able to even think I was thinking rationally, although most people probably thought I had been irrational for months. I didn't know what to do or even how to accomplish the simple instructions I was given. Even breathing seemed awkward. I tried to listen attentively to the doctor and nurses. I convinced myself their reassuring voices would get me through the next minutes, and they did. The doctor said, "On your next contraction, I want you to push really hard." However, I was in such disarray mentally that I was not able to distinguish a contraction from any other feeling in my pulsating body. So I decided to just start pushing and not stop. Not stopping for the head to come out, not stopping for the body to come out, I only stopped when I felt the feet flopping out.

Within thirty minutes of entering the hospital, the birth was over. It was a girl. As I looked at her crying on my stomach, I just thought, *Where are her teeth?* as my muddled thoughts tried to clarify the miracle I was watching.

The afterbirth procedures took forever and were longer and even less romantic than the actual birth. I lay there thinking through the previous hours and thinking through the times of my life when I had imagined that moment. Had giving birth lived up to what I had expected? Yes. I felt overjoyed. I had survived childbirth and had a beautiful, toothless baby girl!

As the doctor stitched me back together, Aaron went to watch Angelica in the nursery. Then he met me in our semiprivate enclave. I desperately wanted a private room, but there had been many births that day, so I had to share. The curtain had been pulled to create a sense of privacy. The conversation was sparse as we watched the *Young and the Restless. We* tried to absorb everything that had happened in the last few hours. Then Aaron's brother reappeared, and our time became filled with comforting small talk. It felt like hours before we were alone again.

When she was finally brought to me, Angelica was perfect. She took naturally to breast-feeding. Our first feeding lasted an hour, and it was wonderful to feel our closeness. When she was satisfied and burped, I handed her over to Aaron. They stared at each other momentarily; recognition bound their very souls. Then, as if to acknowledge the beginning of a lifetime bond, Angelica gave her daddy a large toothless smile. We sat in the silence of the evening after the turmoil of the birth. Aaron held his baby girl, cooing at her as he had done when she was in my womb. Suddenly and spontaneously, Angelica smiled the biggest smile I could imagine. She was recognizing and acknowledging the father who would protect her through life's trials. Some would say it wasn't a smile, only gas. Aaron and I knew differently. We were parents. We were a family. And that day would be the beginning of our lives together. That toothless smile would take us through the trials and tribulations of life.

Home at Last

After years of abundant sleep, I look back on the first few weeks of Angelica's life with fond memories. The continuous feeling of sleep deprivation and the general sense of lethargy created a trance-like, dreamy quality. I felt content with the robotic nature of my daily routine. Except, when nurturing a newborn, this level of outer-body experience generally comes with a large psychiatrist bill and might require numerous antipsychotic drugs or an extended stay at a tropical spa.

When Angelica came home, it was just the three of us: Aaron, Angelica, and me. I was not working outside the home. Unlike many mothers, I had no anxious countdown to the dreaded day when I would have to return to work. I was breast-feeding Angelica a lot. It got to the point where my pediatrician called her feeding "demand feeding."

Although breast-feeding became as innate as breathing, I had mixed feelings. My emotions arose from my multicultural perspective. On one hand, there was my mother—possibly the first feminist on earth. She was definitely the initial woman to banish her bra from her wardrobe in the 1950s. She believed and taught me that breasts were for feeding children anywhere and everywhere they desired. On the other hand, there were my in-laws. They had been brought up below the Baptist Bible Belt in Florida (a stone's throw from the Georgia line). Maybe they descended from slaves who had been required to breast-feed their master's children. My in-laws had never considered the need to breast-feed their children. They believed breast-feeding was a choice. They chose the convenience and liberation of a baby's bottle full of specially designed formula. Nevertheless, I chose breast-feeding.

Before I started breast-feeding Angelica, I had a general sympathy for anyone who would breast-feed her child in public. As my days of breast-feeding turned into weeks and months, my general tolerance turned into clear empathy.

One late Saturday afternoon, I sat in our small living room, preparing to feed Angelica. She fidgeted as usual, not wanting to wait for me to unhook my specially designed bra. I paused for a moment to consider which breast we should start on, wanting to ensure I started where we had finished during our previous feeding.

Angelica attached quickly but fidgeted for a few moments more. The breast was too engorged with milk, making it difficult for her to attach to the flattened nipple and begin sucking. Once I finally helped her attach, her squirms of frustration disappeared. As Angelica gulped warm milk without a moment's hesitation, I wondered whether an adult could keep up with drinking a comparable amount.

I enjoyed watching Angelica suck and suck as she swallowed the warm milk. Then she coughed slightly as the milk flowed more quickly than she anticipated. Finally, she relaxed as the milk began to pour into her mouth. My breast went from a feeling of engorged pain to warm bursts as the milk emptied into Angelica's mouth. From deep inside my breast, I could feel more milk being manufactured from seemingly nothing. What a miracle. I could watch Angelica feeding for what felt like hours, her little feet twitching as if to communicate her satisfaction.

After about twenty minutes, I stuck my finger into her mouth to break her suction and moved her with little protest to the other breast. Within fifteen minutes, she was sleeping more than sucking. Every now and then, just as I would consider removing her from my breast, she would start sucking again as if to tell me she wasn't quite ready to finish. Within thirty minutes, she dropped off my breast, asleep and full of milk, a slight grin on her face. Her contented grin could have stopped wars if only we could have captured it in a bottle and distributed it as a spray across continents.

The biggest surprise once Angelica and I came home from the hospital was the number of diapers needing changed each day. The number averaged thirteen or fourteen. Many days I changed her crib blankets two or three, or even four times as a result of diaper leaks. The brownish-yellowish liquid Angelica produced became our way of communicating. A little round dot in the middle of her diaper: empty stomach, it was time to eat. Brown stains seeping through her outfit from a leak: a hearty meal was being celebrated. I was normally unscathed by these events. Occasionally, even I was surprised by the amount of runny liquid substance collecting in Angelica's diaper, mostly when it smelled similar to a toxic waste dump-even to me, her mother. But most days changing a diaper felt as natural as breast-feeding. (Nevertheless, I recognized the difference.)

I was very lucky not to experience postpartum depression when I brought Angelica home from the hospital. It was one of the most physically and mentally challenging periods of my life. The thought of simultaneously having a state of unhappiness and helplessness was incomprehensible to me. There was only one moment during the first year of Angelica's life when I thought I would lose my mind. It was a point when I thought I might do damage to my precious baby.

Angelica was nearly three months old but did not yet exhibit the affection of that age group. She was never a crier (she was too busy eating), but one afternoon she wouldn't stop screaming. The cry was like a group of twenty first graders dragging their nails slowly and repeatedly down a blackboard while laughing incessantly. The sound magnified as it penetrated further into my exhausted brain. I sat in the living room of our small, twelve-hundred-square-foot home and stared at the wall with hopeless desperation. On the wall, the shadow of a tree from the garden created monster-like figures waiting to devour the both of us. I was starting to imagine that Angelica was crying deliberately to alert me of the lurking evil. I fed her. She cried. I changed her. She cried. I held her. And she cried. I felt completely hopeless and unable to see how I was going to get past that desperate moment. Was it going to be a horrific, defining moment in my life, altering my future? Would I awake wearing a prison-spec, orange jumpsuit rather than the latest ensemble from the Christian Dior spring collection?

Finally I took a deep breath and remembered some words of wisdom I had heard on a talk show: If you need a break from early motherhood, call someone to take your child so you can get some rest. Call someone to help you before you harm your child. As a first-time mother, I was reluctant to call my in-laws. I wanted to prove I was worthy to be called a mother. My own family was an ocean away in England. So instead of calling anyone, I took a deep breath, put Angelica in the center of our queen-sized bed, and left her there while I regained my composure. This potential mistake comes back to me periodically: Angelica could have suffocated in a freak accident. But she didn't. It was a defining decision in my life, a point-of-time intersection. Such intersections can move you on a positive path of growth and understanding or a negative path that can ultimately spiral your life out of control. Fortunately for me, both of us survived the episode without either of us being harmed. And I believe at least one of us was a little wiser as a result of this experience.

* * *

Before Angelica was born, I had a particular fascination with babies' socks. I spent hours wandering around JCPenney looking at baby outfits, particularly socks. Due to the technology of the time, I didn't know the sex of my child, so I generally looked at neutral clothes: green and yellow. It was difficult to believe that my baby would have feet so very small, not even the size of half my thumb. I spent every waking hour waiting for my days to be filled with my baby.

Once Angelica was born, I was unprepared for how restrictive my life would become. Aaron and I spent every available moment together. On weekends we would sleep-in or doze until early afternoon before rolling out of bed for a very late brunch. Lazy Saturdays became filled with parenthood and doctor visits. Angelica's first doctor's visit was at one thirty in the afternoon two weeks after her birth. I started getting prepared at nine o'clock in the morning. Even though I had not put a lot of weight on during my pregnancy, it was difficult to decide what to wear. The prepregnancy clothes were out of the question; it felt as if I would never fit in a size two again. My early pregnancy clothes were not an option because most of them were for the hazy days of a Floridian summer, and it was mid-February. I was also breast-feeding Angelica, so I needed to wear special clothes. They had to unbutton in front allowing easy, but discrete access to Angelica's single source of food: my breasts. They had to be light in color to camouflage my never-ending breast milk leakages. Yes, I had more outfit requirements than an Oscar-nominated actress heading for a front row seat at the Oscars. For the previous two weeks, I had lived in button-up pajamas. I almost wished I could wear them to the doctor's office. In fact, the thought crossed my mind. Then I had another thought: the pediatrician might think I was crazy and lock me up and take Angelica away. With my brain functioning at a primitive level, it took all my effort to pick out a comfortable, practical outfit.

It was ten o'clock in the morning. Before I could shower and get myself ready, Angelica started to cry, wanting to be fed. I spent the next hour bathing her, feeding her, and dressing her in a cute little doctor's outfit I had purchased especially for her first appointment.

By eleven thirty in the morning, I felt as if I was running out of time. I quickly showered and put my clothes on. There was no time for hair and makeup. It was noon, and I needed to leave by twelve thirty. Fortunately, I had prepared Angelica's diaper bag the night before. I had packed enough for a camping trip. In hindsight, I wished I had laid her in the infant car seat to sleep after I had fed her earlier. As I picked Angelica up from her crib, I smelled a familiar odor coming from her diaper. As I investigated, I realized her diaper was full, and a yellowish brown substance had stained her new outfit. It was twelve fifteen. I began to panic. I could feel my heart beat faster in my chest as adrenaline began gushing through my body. What was supposed to be a leisurely drive to the doctor's was turning into a nightmare. I removed Angelica's clothes, washed her with a cloth, and put another set of clothes on her. At that point, cuteness didn't matter. Functionality had taken over. It was time to leave.

It took me another twenty minutes to get Angelica's infant car seat, her diaper bag, and, finally, myself into the car. Deep breath... I had made it! I was only a few minutes late for the appointment, but fortunately, the pediatrician was running even later. No one noticed. I just prayed that practice would make perfect. Otherwise I feared I would have to lower my life goals to just attending Angelica's doctor's appointments for the next eighteen years.

* * *

When Angelica was born, I was still in college. The semester she was born, I decided to take online courses. I took a total of three general education classes. When Angelica was twelve weeks old, it was time to take my final exams. The college had made special accommodations. A separate room allowed me to both take the exam and breast-feed Angelica. I had become quite an expert at leaving with Angelica in less than an hour and a half, often despite Angelica's uncooperative antics. She would demand an additional feeding. She would require an additional change of clothes. Or she would refuse to wait patiently while I dressed. It was as if she knew our schedule was changing without her full endorsement. But to be at the campus by ten o'clock in the morning, I had prepared the night before. We left the house by nine fifteen.

Once we reached the college, we were greeted by a special assistant, who escorted us into an abandoned classroom. In the far corner, a group of four chairs sat under their desks, possibly waiting to welcome four students rather than a mother, child, infant car seat, and large diaper bag. The remaining chairs sat on top of their designated tables, as if preparing for the end-of-day cleaning crew. The assistant was very nice and said I could start whenever I was ready. I thought it sensible to feed and change Angelica first. Within thirty minutes, she was propped up in her car seat, looking curiously at me as I started to scribble. She sat there, patiently watching me, dosing off periodically until my hour was up. I was so proud of us; we had finished our first exam together. We got three As that semester. The idea of joint time started to emerge as an interesting solution to my life's competing priorities. Joint time became times when our overlapping individual needs could be met during the same moments of life.

Soon after we achieved three As in the online classes, we received a call from the local newspaper preparing a story about nontraditional students. The journalist spent fifteen minutes on the phone asking pertinent questions related to my experiences with the first series of on-line courses offered by college (now called Florida State College Jacksonville). Every few minutes Angelica would grunt her support of the program. At the end of the call, the journalist requested a time a photojournalist could take a couple of pictures. The next day the photographer appeared promptly at 3:00 p.m. After formal introductions, he decided to position Angelica and me in front of our large television screen where we watched the college classes. Angelica was sitting on the right side of the screen in her baby seat with a large pink bow stuck to her head. Her chubby cheeks were centered in the middle of the picture frame. I was sitting on the opposite side peering at both the television and my baby girl. I was a very proud mother. After a few snaps, the photographer was gone and Angelica and I decided to take an afternoon nap. I thought little about the event until the next day when I received a call from my husband. We had made the front page of the local newspaper. We were celebrities—at least for that day.

The Road to Emancipation

As much as I desired to have a little person who totally relied on me, within months of Angelica's birth, I craved the reverse. Emancipation came over the first few months of Angelica's life. I felt liberated as my helpless baby started to morph into a child with her own needs and wants that extended beyond eating and sleeping.

The first moment of liberation came when Angelica actually remained awake, looked in my eyes, cooed, and smiled. It was a bright sunny day, and we had just finished one of our long, relaxing feedings. Usually Angelica would be completely relaxed, arms drooping at her sides, every now and again sucking on her tongue. That day she just stared up at me inquisitively, seemingly imprinting every part of my smiling face in her brain. I gazed back, not quite knowing what to do next. Suddenly she started talking in long, sweet sounding utterances. She paused and started smiling. This was a moment that provided me with a lifetime of appreciation and enabled me to continue my self-sacrificing role regardless of frustrations and circumstances.

The next moment of liberation was when Angelica finally slept for more than two and a half seconds in a row. (OK, I am exaggerating just a little.) I was busy completing my chores around the house and noted it was time for Angelica's feeding. I went into her room; she was sleeping angelically on her back, her head turned toward me. Her whole body was in the rhythmical movement of sleep. I could hear the slow sound of her breaths, which was accompanied by the leisurely motions of her chest and the rhythmic twitches of her hands and feet. As a new mother, I hesitated, not quite sure what to do. For weeks, with accounting-like precision, I had been feeding this child every two hours. We were now in the fourth hour of a deep sleep with no signs that Angelica would wake. I was perplexed. What should I do? Instinct (as well as a desire for more time alone) kept whispering, "Let her sleep, let her sleep." I was confused, torn between my selfish desires and motherly practicality. In fact, I was so worried that Angelica was still asleep that I called the doctor to confirm it was acceptable! Patiently, they told me such sleep was normal for Angelica's age. What a relief. Angelica stayed asleep for almost six hours that day, providing another moment in my path to emancipation.

The final moment of complete freedom arrived when Aaron and I started to prepare Angelica to sleep through the night. This preparation required a combination of resilience and earplugs. Our pediatrician said we would need to allow Angelica to wake up at night, change her diaper, and then put her back to bed without additional food or cuddling. As we spent many nights feeling like we were emotionally depriving our only child, it felt as if Angelica would never sleep through the night.

Angelica's chosen night of reckoning happened when Aaron and I had a busy day ahead of us and had decided to collapse into bed straight after Angelica's late-evening feeding. It was a little after ten o'clock, and we were both exhausted. Prepared to be woken by a crying child at any time, we immediately fell asleep.

From deep inside my soul, something tugged me awake. Was it a baby? No, I instinctively didn't think so. Something was pulling me into consciousness. Was it my husband? Had I unconsciously blocked my beautiful baby girl's crying demands? No, at least not that time. It was the morning sun and a chorus of birds acknowledging the beauty of the day. I cautiously looked toward the clock. *I must be dreaming*, I thought. The clock announced seven o'clock. Our house was silent. I looked toward my husband. He slept peacefully beside me, his body silently acknowledging the remarkableness of the situation. Angelica had slept through the night. The moment a newborn sleeps through the night is one of the most magical moments of life. My moment appeared as nature's way of rewarding me for the months of selfless sacrifice. It was a reward superior to any knighting, Oscar, or other honor—a blissful, undisturbed night of sleep.

My prize was accompanied by a sense of triumph, but the joy was suddenly chased away by a sense of panic. I realized we hadn't used our mechanical alarm for the first time in months. We were both late! But it didn't matter—another milestone, possibly the most important last mile in the road to sleep deprivation emancipation, had been reached. After thirteen weeks of not sleeping more than a few hours at a time, I felt so accomplished, refreshed, and exhilarated. Well, at least for that one day and one night.

Chapter Two

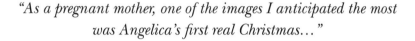

"As a pregnant mother, one of the images I anticipated the most was Angelica's first real Christmas..."

Here Comes the Toddler

After Angelica was born, I studied the developmental book my pediatrician had given me, wanting to know what my baby should accomplish each month. The book gave approximate ages when we should expect certain events to happen. My expectations were that Angelica would achieve her goals well in advance of the published ages. I was coaching Angelica to complete her first push-up onto her arms. I helped her complete her first rolling-over-onto-the-back move. (I kept telling her it's all about the head.) I cheered on the sidelines as she completed her first rolling-back-onto-the-stomach, an even more complex feat.

Angelica was six months old and my baby girl looked like a crafted doll you buy from an upscale doll shop. Her big brown eyes melted my heart away daily. Her large chubby cheeks complemented her doll-like features flawlessly. Twelve faultlessly straight white teeth setoff her adorable smile. We had made it through the first six month of Angelica's life on earth. It was time to celebrate. It was time for Angelica's six-month checkup. I was excited when the doctor authorized Angelica to start eating solid food. We went straight to our favorite local supermarket, Publix, where shopping is a true pleasure. I secured Angelica in her deluxe, portable baby-basket contraption. Her first "solid" food was a very juicy nectarine, and she loved it. Her front teeth took on a whole new role as they pierced the firm but ripe, sweet fruit. The juice attached itself to Angelica's chubby cheeks and hands before it traveled slowly down her plump neck. Rather than acting like a mother and fussing about the sticky mess being created, I felt like a grandmother as I delighted in the nectarine juice seeping down her chest. Large amounts of sticky nectarine juice and pulp started to accumulate on her cheeks. At one point, it appeared as if the nectarine was eating Angelica instead of the other way around.

* * *

Angelica was thirteen months old, and to maintain her pattern of true genius behavior, she should have been walking. It was time to catch up. It was a Sunday night, and we were practicing her walking. I would put Angelica a couple of feet away on the blue, overly padded carpet, not far from her crib. I would balance Angelica as we held on to each other, dark brown eyes gazing into dark brown eyes. Then I would slowly let go of her, and she would slowly let go of me. I would shift myself backward, keeping an eye on Angelica as she looked directly at my extended hands. I called her. Angelica started running to me, giggling, only just making it before she fell into my arms. We practiced again and again, never wearying of the moments, minutes, or hours that cool Sunday evening.

Angelica didn't walk that night. This was the moment when she *almost* learned to walk. She crossed the threshold from a crawler to a walker. The actual moment she walked has been lost from my memory.

Potty Training with a Purpose

Some mothers like to claim their successes based on the classes their children are taking in high school or the universities their children are attending. For me, potty training is the first real milestone to confirm a mother's true greatness.

When it came to potty training, my grade was probably a depressing D- that was elevated to a B- based on society's norms. This was my first child—everything *had* to be right! Potty training was a way of validating my womanhood. I even dreamed of becoming a dinner-table expert at our ritualistic family functions. Everything appeared new and exciting. Okay, maybe I was actually seeing potty training through rose-colored, romanticized glasses, but I still imagined the family accolades I would receive if I was successful in the task. Maybe it would be the initial validation that my child was a genius on the level of Albert Einstein. (Only the story goes that Albert Einstein wasn't potty trained at an early age either!)

Due to the importance of potty training in both Angelica's life and mine, I endeavored to identify the leading experts and tools in the field. I realized the importance of being well educated and equipped. The proper wisdom and guidance would be paramount to ensure victory. I achieved all this through a marvelous entity that is miraculously accessible in most cities. There is no membership required to use their expertise. They even have a means for you to purchase the necessary equipment needed. I headed to Babies "R" Us. After several hours of research, I made purchases that included a potty I could place on top of the toilet, a couple of books, the latest style of toddler underwear, and special reward snacks in the shape of various toiletries. Despite a large deficit in my bank account, I was ready.

Although many of my memories of potty training Angelica are a bit of a blur, there are a couple that continue to resonate as if they are branded in my memory. When Angelica was being potty trained, I had transferred to the University of North Florida (UNF) to complete my bachelor's degree. They had a nursery on the campus, and I passed it daily. The grounds looked so welcoming, like a land of fruit and honey. I thought the nursery was the place where my daughter could have unfathomable fun. Furthermore, using the on-campus nursery would allow me to set aside the guilt of being away from her. There were two barriers to entry into that quasi-Disneyland: Angelica *had* to be two years old *and* potty trained. When I started at the UNF, Angelica was eighteen months old and not potty trained. And so our six-month adventure began. Well, almost, because Angelica's birthday was in January, and the next college nursery class would not begin until August. Angelica would be two and a half.

Just for the record, Angelica was generally not cooperative in our potty training adventure. I tried to keep her underwear on most of the time during the day. (Back then they didn't have the potty-training diapers available today.) To ensure success in the task, it required frequent, almost obsessive trips to the bathroom. Every two hours I would lug her to the bathroom, oftentimes under her protests, sometimes with her cooperation.

The first time I pulled her underwear down, she obediently climbed the stairs of her toilet, perching triumphantly on top. Her face beamed with satisfaction. She had a loving smile on her face and her saucer-sized eyes looked up at me. As time passed, she began chattering to me. Her questioning bled into the late afternoon as she continued to sit on the toilet. I cautiously turned on the tap, hoping to speed up the natural flow of things. Then, suddenly, there was a sound that ignited the "Hallelujah Chorus" in my brain! I could hear a slow and steady flow of urine hitting the toilet water. I was determined to contain my delight, concerned it would stall progress. I politely applauded her success while I inwardly leaped for joy.

That one success was followed by less successful patterns of behavior. Most of the time I would coax her to the bathroom every other hour and pull down her pants as she wriggled in disobedience. Generally, if she protested, I was too late; the pants were already wet. After weeks, possibly months, we reached a point when she acknowledged understanding this ritual.

One day I was looking for Angelica. I found her perched on her potty seat, which sat on the toilet in our only bathroom. She had missed some small details, such as the fact that she should have pulled her underwear down. But she got it! This was the initial sign of hope. Or at least she knew that if I found her sitting on the toilet, I would be happy and maybe she would get a treat.

Once, Angelica, her "grown-up underwear," and I took a quick trip to the grocery store to pick up some important items for dinner. I stood in front of a shelf full of a thousand varieties of salad dressings, entranced by the available selection. Angelica sat in the top part of the basket. She was perfectly positioned so she could incessantly talk to me while grabbing salad dressings easily accessible from her well-positioned chair. I don't remember her asking anxiously to use the bathroom. Abruptly I heard the sound of water dripping. My first thought was that Angelica had broken a bottle of salad dressing. *Was she hurt?* I thought. My brain readjusted as I realized the sound was more like a liquid. I wondered whether there was a leak in the roof. Instantaneously I realized it came from under Angelica. But the liquid wasn't just hitting the floor. First it dripped onto the basket bottom, then to the rack, and then to the floor. For each drop I heard a rhythmic *drip-drip* as every bead of water hit the lower parts of the basket twice. That was followed by the sound of a steady flow of liquid hitting the floor. *How much did Angelica drink?* I wondered. The flow seemed endless.

When we had initially turned down the aisle, it was empty other than Angelica and me. In slow motion, I looked from side to side as the liquid continued to pitter-patter to the ground. I hoped we were still alone on the aisle. I thought, *What shall I do? Shall I continue shopping? Run out of the store? Chastise Angelica? Go to the bathroom and command she complete her remaining activity there?* Instead, I requested assistance from a nearby shelf stocker. The stocker called customer service, which in turn announced to the whole store, "Bill, there's a cleanup on aisle seven."

The stocker appeared within minutes, well equipped for the task at hand. He was holding a mop in one hand and pulling a bucket full of dark water that smelled of disinfectant with the other. "Thanks, Bill," I heard myself saying moments later. "We are potty training, and we had a little accident." He nodded as if this was not his first accident cleanup of the day.

Well, the accidents got less frequent, even if they didn't get less embarrassing. Angelica was finally accepted by the campus nursery school. Unfortunately, this was followed by a period of regressive potty-training behavior. My main worry was that Angelica would be expelled from the nursery school right after getting accepted, but she wasn't. In fact, it became a pretty regular occurrence that I would drop Angelica off with a change of clothes (sometimes two) and pick her up at the end of the day with a companion—a neatly tied bag of soiled clothes.

Angelica was more than two and a half when we finally finished potty training. It was quite an accomplishment if I do say so myself.

Bedtime

As an only child with a growing family, there were daily times when I needed my space. This need to be left alone was usually magnified close to bedtime. At that time my ability to clearly judge right from wrong, good from bad, and rebellion from compliance, was fuzzy.

Angelica was never a great sleeper as a toddler. You could put her to bed at eight o'clock then peek into her room at eleven o'clock and she would be sitting wide-eyed on her bed, fiddling with her latest toy. The only solace I had was that ultimately the good evened out the bad. Angelica, if allowed, could sleep until midmorning, and she loved to take long afternoon naps. Some mothers might recommend cutting out the nap. Not me! Even if Angelica got up early and skipped the nap, she always had trouble falling asleep at night, and my day was made agonizing due to a grumpy, non-cooperative toddler.

With all Angelica's shenanigans at bedtime, one night of trauma stands out. Angelica was still sleeping in her crib. Nevertheless, she could quickly, with a certain degree of agility, propel herself over the crib's bars and slip unhurt to the ground. It was a particularly hot night in the tropical climate of Florida, and Angelica was thirty-two months old. We had had an exciting day full of water games, candy, and summer fun. As usual on Saturday nights, Aaron and I cuddled on the sofa. We had just put Angelica to bed, and we were planning a movie night. We would all sleep in the next day.

At five minutes after nine, Angelica wandered into the living room and said, "Mummy, I need a glass of water. I am thirsty."

I said, "Angelica, go to sleep."

She reappeared ten minutes later. "Daddy, I need a glass of water, I am thirsty."

Aaron said, "Angelica, please get a small glass of water, use the restroom, and then go to bed."

At half past nine, Angelica finally said, "Thank you, Daddy, I am going to bed. I love you both."

"Goodnight, Angelica," we said.

By ten o'clock, Angelica realized I was past the hour of being able to say anything other than "no" and "go to bed." So she went to Aaron and said, "Daddy, I need to use the restroom."

Lowering his voice, Aaron said, "Angelica, go use the restroom. Then, *go* to bed."

"It's a number two, Daddy."

Aaron's voice softened slightly. "Okay," he said. "Finish and then go to bed."

Angelica came back twenty minutes later. "I'm done, Daddy."

"Okay, then go to bed."

She stayed away until ten forty-five. "Daddy, I can't sleep."

Aaron got up and went to tuck his little girl into bed. I am not sure what was said, but everything was right with the world at that moment. I heard the muffled sounds of father and daughter talking and agreeing on a plan of action. The house settled into a pleasant, quiet slump.

At least until a quarter after eleven. "Daddy, it didn't work. I can't sleep."

"Angelica, go to sleep," Aaron said. "Close your eyes and go to sleep."

The ritual continued for a couple more hours before it started to escalate. Aaron's voice became louder, and his hand prepared to spank a tiny bottom. By one o'clock in the morning, the whole house had lost its sense of repose. Everyone was tired. I felt a sense of desperation. Even our dog requested to be let into the garden, where she then stayed all night. Angelica was exhausted and in a state of hysteria. Aaron got up from the couch and moved apprehensively toward Angelica's bedroom. He decided it was time to end the drama. I finally heard sobbing from Angelica's room. Within minutes, her sobs changed to protests as Angelica continued to defy the bodily urge to sleep. Finally, other than the sound of the early morning birds, there was silence.

The night after Angelica couldn't sleep, we all slept well. We woke up the next morning (or should I say afternoon), refreshed and ready for the day. Nothing was said about the event. The only memories that remain are mine, along with a sense of guilt for not being able to calm Angelica down earlier.

Oh, the Messes

One thing that is guaranteed is that children will make messes. There are various kinds of messes: planned and unplanned, funny, absolute, and ultimate. They usually come at the worst moments, testing a mother's self-control. For me, a professed perfectionist, disarray invading my impeccably clean and ordered world was inconvenient, tiresome, and inopportune. There have been many chaotic moments over the years, but certain ones stand out. What is the relationship that threads them together? Oh…the mess.

Immediately upon Angelica's birth, I started envisioning her bedroom: a princess's room, pink, pretty, and with plenty of ruffled trimmings. Aaron and I didn't have much additional cash when it was time to change Angelica's room from a baby's to a little girl's room. Consequently, I looked for months for the ideal second-hand princess furniture at the lowest price. I found it, a beautiful, white canopy bed with pink trimming and a matching nightstand and dressing table. As a bonus, the couple we bought the furniture from gave us the accompanying bedding. Aaron repainted the furniture and tightened up several loose screws. We had decided on pink for her bedroom walls (of course), but I didn't accompany Aaron to Home Depot. When he came home with bright pink paint, I had to decide between criticism and compliments. I opted for compliments, and after an undercoat, Aaron began painting Angelica's room pink…*bright* pink.

Aaron started early on a Saturday morning, and the room was ready before Angelica's bedtime. I was so excited about putting Angelica to bed that night. It seemed like the culmination of a dream. Angelica, wearing her new Cinderella nightclothes, curled up under her new bedspreads. I perched on the side of the bed and read her favorite Disney tale. Before long, I kissed her, Daddy kissed her, and the light was switched off. Within minutes, Angelica fell asleep.

The next evening our regular routine continued. Before long it was time for Angelica to go to bed. She had been playing in her room by herself most of the evening. I bounced into her room and looked at her beautiful canopy bed; one of the poles was bent, as if someone had been swinging on it. Red punch stained the matching bedspread. Writing (scribbling? art?) decorated the freshly painted walls. I would like to remember counting to ten, sighing, and preparing for daddy's response. So that's how I will remember that muddle. Oh, the mess.

Angelica was also great at organizing her messes. When Angelica was two or three, I worked weekends as a waitress. That left Aaron and Angelica to take care of each other in my absence. Sometimes I didn't know who was looking after whom. One Saturday, Aaron took a late afternoon nap on the comfortable couch in our living room. He was startled by the phone, jumped up to answer it, and fell. When he recovered his composure, he noticed the crayons, which had been broken in half and meticulously organized in a pattern that covered the whole living-room floor. Aaron said he could barely see the floor. Then he heard Angelica saying, "Hello? Yes. No. He's asleep on the sofa. Daddy, it's for you." Aaron answered the phone to find that not only had Angelica been busy redecorating, but she had also been busy calling 911.

Three police cars were on the way, which was the customary procedure when 911 was called three times without a response at the other end. Oh, the messes.

Angelica also had a special ability to cultivate her messes until they created special odors generally only found in garbage dumps. Angelica had a deluxe kitchen set in her room. She loved washing dishes, baking cakes, and cooking magnificent breakfasts. I have never had the best sense of smell, especially when compared to my husband, who can smell something rotting on the other side of the neighborhood. Early one day I noticed a slight odor in Angelica's room. I looked under the bed, inside her drawers, and in her closet, but I couldn't locate the smell. Every day it got a little worse.

By Friday I was recruiting Aaron to locate the source of the offending odor. As a United States Marine, surely he was trained to focus on this type of mission. Failure was not an option. He stood at the entrance of the room and sniffed toward the bed, the night-stand, the dressing table, and, lastly, the closet. His nose and his body systematically zeroed in on the enemy smell. His nose instinctively hovered in the direction of the deluxe kitchen set. He made a puzzled look on his face, as if this was a familiar odor. In a few minutes, he called me. He opened the deluxe kitchen set. In the center of the oven was an unfamiliar container. Aaron recognized it. The bowl held his favorite auntie's homemade seafood salad, which had been missing from our refrigerator for about a week. Aaron had presumed I had thrown the container out during one of my compulsive cleaning sprees. Fortunately, the pungent odor barely seeped from under the well-sealed lid. But even the small odor seeping out was bad. Really bad. Oh, the mess.

Extracurricular Activities

Even when children are only twinkles in their American parents' eyes, I believe their extracurricular activities are already predestined. Particular sports appear to be passed down from generation to generation. Oftentimes a parent's childhood memories are clear. The desire to either replicate or fix those memories, whatever the case may be, is strong and possibly biological. My memories were of piano, violin, ballet, tap dancing (with my mummy), and endless hours at the park. And so that is how Angelica's activities started. We were lucky enough that gymnastics, ballet, and swimming were offered at Angelica's nursery school.

My sweetest memories of Angelica at three years old were her first, and most probably her second, third, fourth, and fifth swimming lessons. We had completed the obligatory water baby classes before Angelica turned six months old. Now it was time for Angelica to learn to swim. I was still in college, and Angelica continued to attend the on-campus nursery. As with many universities, there was a state of the art swimming facility. The pool the nursery school used was on campus and appeared larger than an Olympic-sized pool to me. It probably seemed even bigger to a two-year-old who had only seen backyard, inflatable pools before. Like most first-time mother's, I was determined that my little girl would be the first to get in the water and learn to swim. Fortunately, the swimming instructor was used to mothers of "my kind." She promptly thanked me for dropping Angelica off and recommended that I come back in an hour. Inwardly I wanted to protest. I was outwardly obedient and left for an hour of necessary chores.

I spent an hour dreaming of the accolades I would receive upon my return. How Angelica was built for swimming. How she took naturally to the water. How I should consider getting her private lessons. And how she truly had Olympic talent. When I returned, all the other children were clothed but displayed evidence of wetness: rag-tail hair, drops of water running down their faces, and slightly damp clothes. Angelica was perfectly dry. She clung to the hand of her favorite teacher, Ms. Sarah. Ms. Sarah came bouncing over to me, Angelica obediently trailing. As Ms. Sarah got closer, she started a stream of empty accolades about how Angelica had put her bathing suit on first and listened to the safety instructions best. My mind jumped ahead of Ms. Sarah's conversation; it couldn't decide whether Angelica had swum like a fish or possibly not. Ms. Sarah went on to say that Angelica had walked around the pool for an hour, familiarizing herself with the surroundings and pondering the task of getting into the pool. I appreciated Ms. Sarah's kindness and patience in allowing Angelica to acclimate slowly to the pool. I smiled and thanked Ms. Sarah. I picked up my baby girl, hugged her, and congratulated her on completing her first official swimming lesson. Or should I have commended her on her first mile walk around the perimeter of the pool. If Angelica wasn't going to be an Olympic swimmer, then perhaps she would be an Olympic track and field star instead.

Angelica's First Real Christmas

As a pregnant mother, one of the images I anticipated the most was Angelica's first real Christmas—a Christmas where Angelica would wake up excited and eager to open the gifts she would receive from Father Christmas (called Santa Clause in the United States). When Angelica was only weeks away from turning four, she had her first real Christmas, and it revolved around her love of playground swings. Aaron and I had gone to Toys "R" Us together, which was always a mistake. Together we imagined big—really big— Christmases, which was usually followed by tossing our budget plans out the figurative window as we got into the Christmas spirit.

It was a few days before Christmas, and only the deluxe versions of all children's toys remained available. That year, it was the deluxe swing set with double slides, swings at every imaginable height, and extra gadgets to entertain and delight. Of course, deluxe also meant it had many very similar pieces to put together. Once we had carefully deposited the unassembled swing set (and many other recklessly purchased gifts) in our large, brown van, we headed home. We could feel the excitement, already anticipating the images of thrill and delight as Angelica saw the swing set for the first time.

First Aaron had to put the swing set together in the back-yard, right outside Angelica's bedroom. Somehow this less than quiet task had to be completed without her knowing about it, even though it was already two thirty in the afternoon on a wintry Christmas Eve. It took Aaron about an hour and a half to unpack all of the pieces, organize them, read the instructions (I hoped), and then organize everything in a manner that would allow easy assembly. Soon it was dinnertime—time to break for our tradi-tional Christmas Eve dinner of grilled cheese sandwiches and the like.

Before Aaron could start again, neighborhood men and Aaron's brother started to gather in the backyard. I imagined they sensed the challenge of a complex task that might require male bond-ing and camaraderie. It was getting late, sunlight was gone, and artificial light flooded the yard. Periodic sounds of banging came from the backyard. I wondered if our neighbors were telling their kids, "Mr. Kendrick is commissioned to help Father Christmas this year." Or were they also trying to keep their own children preoc-cupied as they counted down to bed?

Soon Angelica was asleep. The banging continued. At some minutes past ten o'clock, Aaron came in, exhausted, a brooding look on his face. "Are you finished?" I asked.

"No," he said simply.

In the morning we guided Angelica into the backyard. She peered around the yard at the opposite end from the newly assembled swing set. My gaze was transfixed on her face as her eyes searched for the Christmas surprise. Her expression changed from being puzzled and curious to complete shock as her eyes fixed on the swing set. Her excitement was more than I could bear. That moment has lasted me through many days of moth-erly frustration. And her only comment as she slid down the slide was "Mummy, Daddy said Santa didn't have time to put the whole swing set together because he had other children's gifts to deliver.

Santa left some of the swing for Daddy to put together. Daddy, when are you going to put the rest of the swing set together?"

Daddy looked at his baby girl with a knowing, slightly tired, smiling face. "Later, baby" is all he could get out. And later it was. Much later. Angelica, now an adult, still remembers this Christmas as her best Christmas ever!

The "swing set Christmas" was a success, primarily because it was before Angelica was able to dream up her own wish list of toys based on the latest commercials or pictures in the JCPenney Christmas catalog. The case of the purple Beauty and the Beast bag was an entirely different story.

It was Christmas Eve, weeks before Angelica would turn five, and I had completed Angelica's Christmas shopping several days earlier. I was without Aaron, therefore less prone to spontaneous gift buying. Angelica was with me as we browsed through the local discount store. Then, without warning, Angelica saw a bag. It wasn't just any bag. It was an authentic Beauty and the Beast bag from the latest movie, and it was obviously the latest rage. I lingered a little as Angelica played with the maze of movie-related paraphernalia. Soon Angelica was tired, and we were able to leave the store with a few necessities such as wrapping paper and tape.

The next morning, as all Christmas mornings, everyone was up early, no matter how late they had stayed up assisting Father Christmas. Angelica was a well-attuned little girl by this time, and she homed in on all her gifts in the living room. As she systematically opened her array of gifts, she kept saying, "I know this is the Beauty and the Beast bag I wanted." After she'd said this a couple of times, my husband looked at me with a questioning glance. As the only male in the house at the time, he relied on me to determine the appropriate gifts for his little princess. Had I failed? How could I have missed the toy she had to have, even though her almost manic desire had started less than eighteen hours earlier? Well, the very next day (sometime after Pic 'N Save opened) there was a final gift found hidden underneath the Christmas tree. Angelica started slowly to unwrap the final hidden gift, a skeptical look on her face. Her whole body communicated her displeasure: this was not the Beauty and the Beast bag she wanted! But it was. She grinned, jumped up, and gave me a large, loving hug. The magic of Christmas was reignited for another instance that year.

Chapter Three

"Finally we both stopped caring about her piano lessons, and I just stopped taking her."

The Arrival of True Childhood

One lesson I have learned the hard way is that young children are tenacious, free-willed characters. In the South, they call it "hard headed," in England "stubborn." Usually this tenacity presents itself at the most inopportune times. I always applaud parents who are able to present their young children in pageants, plays, and recitals. However, my memories of Angelica's debut performances generally have an audience of one—me.

Angelica was about two at the time of her true debut performance. I was attending the UNF, trying to decide whether to change my major from labor-intensive chemistry to accounting. Angelica still attended the very progressive child development center on campus while I went to class or studied. One late summer afternoon, we were on campus, walking down a long, outside concrete hallway. All I could hear was the *click-clack* of my high-heeled shoes and the rhythmic thump of my heavy backpack as it hit a metal piece of my belt. Angelica was a few steps ahead of me and had a little more of a bounce in her step than usual. I kept urging her to slow down because my heels just couldn't keep up with the increasing pace of her quick steps. I am not sure what Angelica heard, but I imagine the director in her head must have said, "Action."

Before I knew it, Angelica was jogging and then an all-out sprint. She appeared to have no specific destination in mind, just a devious motive as she accelerated away from me. I scuttled along with my backpack, trying to imagine how I was going to catch that three-foot laughing munchkin before she reached the busy parking lot. The scene must have been funny from afar: a young woman in a coordinated, bright colored top and shorts with matching high-heeled shoes, trying to maintain her breath and composure while carrying a thirty-pound book bag and chasing after a small child half her size.

"Cut," I imagined the director in Angelica's head said. "Cut."

Angelica stopped running, looked back at me, and giggled. I pretended not to be out of breath even though sweat ran down my forehead. I slowed to a relaxed, uninterested but alert pace, as if I was a lioness cornering a frightened deer. Yet in this case, the deer was happy to continue the game.

Once I grabbed Angelica's small, cool hand, I tried to chastise my beloved baby girl. Of course it was difficult to chastise someone who looked up at me with big brown eyes and a little smirk on her face, and who obviously believed she was in the movie *Catch Me If You Can*.

By the time *Catch Me If You Can 2* came out, I was no wiser to the plot than I was for the original production. This time we were in a grocery store, and I didn't have heels on. Suddenly the director in Angelica's head shouted, "Action!" And she was gone. She flew down aisle seven and turned onto aisle eight, which held all the breakable plates and glasses. My mind presented a picture of Angelica sliding into a shelf of glasses. The picture changed to Angelica lying on the floor surrounded by broken glasses and plates. The image changed again as sound entered the picture: Angelica's initial silent shock giving way to loud sobs. *Was she all right?* My brain was asking. I consciously anticipated the actual sound of a massive collision and the potential damage to the store—glass, plastic, and silverware everywhere. By the time I got to the end of the aisle and turned the corner, there was Angelica, caught in the arms of an old, wise policeman who had seen her taking off and caught her as she rounded the bend. I thanked him graciously, tapped Angelica on the bottom, and scolded her. Then I quickly picked her up, put her in the basket, and buckled her tightly in.

Little did I know that as true childhood arrived, the whole world would become a stage for Angelica. Lights! Action!

To Have Pets or Not to Have Pets: That Should Be a Mother's Decision

As a child, I had a small menagerie of pets. Life hadn't turned out for my mummy and me as she had expected. Mummy had divorced from the man she presumed would be her lifelong companion, and I was an only child. When I turned seven, Mummy became sick, never quite regaining her health. We started buying animals when I was eight, adding to our four-member family: Mother, our two cats—Kitty and Peking—and me. I believe we both found solace in animals, a place to hide from the harshness of life and the uncertainty of the future. Pets provided unconditional love. They required a schedule and a consistent routine. While the erratic nature of illness brought insecurity, the constant needs of pets brought refuge and safety. We were introduced to rabbits then guinea pigs. These were followed by birds (parakeets and finches), two tortoises, two rats (Françoise and Juliette, who had sixteen babies), a miniature owl, and a series of additional cats (generally due to procreation). We never had a dog. Our rationale—a dog would be impossible to handle in an apartment! Besides, we were cat people.

When I married, I was "animaled out." I had a deep love and respect for animals, but after years of constant feeding, cleaning, and grooming, the thought of having another pet was absurd. Anyway, I wasn't so convinced that pets taught children responsibility (although it had for me). I thought it would only result in another chore. Then a stray Siberian husky appeared at my mother-in-law's house (or at least that's what my husband told me).

Aaron had been brought up with dogs. He was a dog man. I was a cat gal. They say opposites attract! When I first saw "Jeanne" (for some strange reason, we named our dog after my mother, and yes, it was my idea), she was at our house. A collar around her neck declared our address as her home. Jeanne had her own little bed. Her own special dishes sat next to the dining room table. Jeanne had moved into our little home. I had only been gone for three hours, and another woman had moved into my house. This was definitely a man with the dog he already loved.

When we moved to the Netherlands for Aaron's work, Jeanne accompanied us. Aaron left for Europe about six months before the rest of us. This gave him enough time to find an apartment and a school for Angelica. It gave me enough time to finish another semester of graduate school. Our house was pretty lonely without Aaron. The three of us—Angelica, Jeanne, and I—drew comfort from each other. Before long, there was an opportunity to add a beautiful black kitten with a white spot on her chest to our family. Angelica decided to call her Arial after the then-popular Disney character.

One day I received an excited call from Angelica while I was in the bedroom. Generally, these calls were for Angelica to announce something very significant to her but probably less noteworthy to me. I finished what I was doing then walked quickly to the sound of Angelica's voice. She was encircled by Jeanne and Arial. Both pets sat comfortably in her lap, looking mournfully up at her as if waiting for further instructions. Angelica proceeded to tell me how she had taught Jeanne to eat cat food and Arial to eat dog food. As she rambled on, I tried to look extremely interested in her achievement, but I could only think, *What will this do to each animal's toilet habits tonight?*

When we finally left for the Netherlands, we had already decided Jeanne was going to accompany us. Arial would remain for my dear sister-in-law, Sherry, to support. After all, Aaron was a dog person!

On the journey over, Jeanne had to be placed in the luggage compartment. During every leg of our journey, and before she considered anything else, Angelica eagerly peered out of either the window of the plane or airport to ensure Jeanne was safely onboard or off. On the initial leg of our journey, we waited at the large window next to the plane, seeing if we could recognize any of our special luggage. Angelica finally saw what she was looking for: Jeanne's large, beige container with a big red bow on top. Angelica triumphantly acknowledged to me and whoever was willing to listen that Jeanne was safely onboard the plane. I could see the dichotomy of traveling passengers' opinions as they either acknowledged Angelica's excitement or became irritated as the ambiance of the crowded airport was interrupted by an excited five-year-old spotting her dog.

Kindergarten Pranks

Living in the Netherlands was comparable to living in the United States in the fifties. Life moved at a much slower pace. Since we lived in the Netherlands, I have a whole new sense of respect for immigrants to America, where English is their second language. Angelica's kindergarten days were spent in a Dutch Catholic kindergarten. I was an Americanized, black, English-speaking protestant. This made for many interesting stories.

When we were there, many mothers did not work in the Netherlands. Most children attended their neighborhood schools. With no school bus transportation and minimal cars, mothers either walked or rode their bikes as they picked up or dropped off their children. The mothers would often congregate outside the school as they waited. The scene was a pleasant picture: mothers laughing, joking, and enjoying each other's company, with no need to count the minutes of a hard-pressed schedule.

On one of those days, a cool autumn breeze blew. I had arrived a little late, and I stood listening to the groups of mothers conversing around me. I tried to listen intently to the conversations, rationalizing that it would benefit my less-than-good comprehension of Dutch. As always, I positioned myself just outside the conversation, hoping and praying that I would not be pulled into the incomprehensible discussion. On this particular day, I observed the usual activity as children appeared in colorful coats, hats, and mittens from the school's front doors. The scene was always the same—children would pause for a moment, gazing into the sea of friendly faces, hoping to spot their mothers. They would start looking exactly in the opposite direction of their mothers, who always stood in deep conversation with the other mothers. The scene never changed. Most days I would observe these events intensely, forgetting that I wasn't just watching a movie.

That day, as the movie-like scene came to an end, I was jolted back to reality when Angelica didn't appear. I waited patiently, mentally rationalizing her lateness. As mothers and their children disappeared, my patience turned to irritation. How many times had I told Angelica not to make me wait? As the last duos left, I walked up to the teacher observing the departing students; my feeling changed from annoyance to bewilderment. The teacher looked at me inquisitively. A sense of panic came on my face as a thousand, horrible, Americanized scenarios flooded my mind. Then I pulled back to reality. The teacher was telling me that Angelica had gone home with her friend. Angelica had said she had my permission.

I thanked the teacher and tried to hide my perplexed look. Mixed feelings welled up in me as I approached Angelica's friend's house, which was two minutes from the school. I felt blessed I lived in a village where everyone knew everybody else (particularly who your child had departed school with that day). But I also felt anger. Why had Angelica left? How many times had I told her about this very scenario? What if she was assaulted? "What ifs" flooded my brain as I knocked on the friend's door. The mother answered with a knowing look on her face. Angelica peeked from behind the mother's skirt. A flood of questions poured from my mouth, my anger contained despite the less than meaningful answers Angelica provided.

Once we left our friend's house to walk home, I began verbally retracing the events; in return, Angelica remained silent. Regretfully, I knew Angelica's punishment must fit her crime. That evening Angelica experienced one of the few spankings she would ever receive, and I hoped it would be memorable enough to keep her safe in the future.

Although it may seem strange, I vividly remember only one of Angelica's teachers—her Dutch kindergarten teacher, Ms. Jansen. Ms. Jansen personally cared about all her students and their families. Ms. Jansen constantly welcomed both Angelica and me with open arms. We had lived in the Netherlands for about six months. Despite daily lessons, my Dutch was coming along agonizingly slowly. Angelica picked up Dutch much quicker. However, Ms. Jansen knew that for her pupil's continued advancement, I must speak Dutch fluently, too. So Ms. Jansen insisted on speaking to me in Dutch. Whenever Ms. Jansen spoke, I listened, stunned anyone babbling so quickly could actually be communicating anything a human brain would understand. I tried to catch every tenth word and piece together her potential question or statement. Then I'd answer in pidgin Dutch as she encouraged me with every word I uttered. Sometimes, her message would be important enough that she conversed with me in perfect English. These seemingly urgent messages were always welcomed into my brain, unrestricted by the demands of intensive brain-babble translation. Within a few months, Angelica was bilingual and became my translator with the teacher. Ms. Jansen would babble rapidly and smile at me, waiting on my slow, jumbled reply. I would look down at my five-year-old as I spoke, waiting for Angelica to signal my answer's correctness. As the teacher's patient smile continued, Angelica innocently coached me through each word. A feeling of incompetence often overwhelmed my emotions as my daughter excelled and I lagged behind in that new, unintelligible world. It was definitely a humbling experience.

Extracurricular Activities Revisited

I have always had reverence for those American parents who take an active role in their children's extracurricular activities. When I grew up in England, most sporting activities for a working class family were completed during school. I had no family tradition related to sports. As a result, the fathers who coached their children's soccer teams, studied new plays, and organized week-end-long trips to regional events seemed superhuman. Mothers who dedicated time to the design and sewing of an entire football team's clothes and then agreed to clean the uniforms weekly, even after rainy, muddy games, deserved the mothers-of-the-year award.

Unfortunately for Angelica, that was not me. Where I excelled was in getting my child to her activities on time and in the right uniforms. I was almost obsessive. It was in that spirit of American tradition that Angelica started taking piano lessons (no teams to coach or uniforms to sew). Angelica started piano with a family friend. Lessons were held in the friend's parlor, and when you entered, you could almost feel yourself stepping back into the 1960s. The parlor was neat and well groomed, with bright carpets, colorful walls, and furniture trapped in sensible plastic coverings. People dropped in and out, picking up their children, waiting on their lessons, and stopping by to pay monies they owed. All the activities occurred in a jovial, relaxed atmosphere. There wasn't a care in the world.

Angelica was six when she started lessons, which she enjoyed. Ms. McFadden was kind and patient and the lessons were easy for Angelica. Angelica quickly learned scales and a few beginning songs. Even daily practices at home were accomplished with only slight signs of resistance.

At the end of each school year, Ms. McFadden held a recital at Friendship Baptist Church. Angelica wore her Easter dress for her first recital. The dress was gorgeous on her—thick cream material, long-sleeved with gold embroidery trim, and a gorgeous, gold-layered net petticoat underneath. I always took pride in the creative styles Angelica wore her hair, and this time she had a series of delicate plaits tied with two golden ribbons into two very cute ponytails. My heart beat rapidly as Angelica was announced and entered stage right. She moved timidly toward the large grand piano, barely peeking up to confirm that Aaron, her auntie, and I sat in the audience. I don't even remember hearing her play. The sound of my heartbeat and the feeling of sweat beads on my forehead overrode any outside stimuli. After what seemed like a century, I was standing, applauding vigorously, and shouting bravo. Then it was over. Angelica bowed, and the next musician appeared.

After the performance, we greeted her with flowers. Life was good.

Over time, I would reflect on Angelica's practice sessions, or lack of practice sessions, and wonder what I could do to ignite a passion for composition, music, and the piano. *As a mother, what should I do differently? Should I demand she practice even when she has no desire? Can I create a love for music in my daughter?*

Angelica took piano lessons for seven years. However, about half-way through, we started battling over her practices. Ms. McFadden insisted her students practice at least thirty minutes a day during the school year. I ensured Angelica adhered to the schedule. When Angelica was ten, her practices started to become a clash of wills. My mind resolved Angelica would practice. Her talent clearly showed that with the right focus she could one day complete the Julliard School and become a professional pianist. Her mind said she was bored and the piano stuff was not her cup of tea. On the inevitable day, I told her to sit down and practice as usual. The keyboard sat in the corner of the dining room, which opened into the kitchen. Generally, I would listen as Angelica started with her scales then moved into the various songs she was supposed to practice that week. However, recently she had barely made it through the scales, stopping and starting every time she missed a note, twisting and turning in her seat. This particular day I could tell we were in for a battle. As usual, I told Angelica it was time to practice. Without arguing, she proceeded to the keyboard and slumped into the seat. I was busy preparing dinner. After a few minutes, I realized I hadn't heard the first note, let alone a scale. Angelica stared stubbornly at the white wall, willing to sit and do nothing for thirty minutes rather than practice. I started a long loud rant that caused my heart to flutter in my chest and my level of frustration to rise quickly. With hindsight on this and many similar occasions, Angelica was becoming the puppeteer, pushing my buttons and waiting on a response, indifferent to the actual response she received.

I decided to try another tactic—learning the piano myself. Then we tried changing teachers. But ultimately nothing modified Angelica's lack of passion. Finally, we both stopped caring about her piano lessons, and I just stopped taking her. Several months later, I bumped into Ms. McFadden. Ms. McFadden asked how Angelica was doing, but the topic of lessons never reared its ugly head.

* * *

Angelica started getting bikes for Christmas at the ripe old age of three. Of course, they were not just bikes but fashion and status symbols, too. Angelica always had a variation of a pink bike: a light pink and yellow, super-Snow White bike; a purple and pink Beauty and the Beast bike; a pink, deluxe Barbie bike with tassels and glitter; and, of course, the supreme Cinderella bike with its own satchel and matching water bottle. The first two or three bikes all had training wheels, and most of the bikes came as part of Christmas-buying extravaganzas. Usually a new bike would be ridden for several hours during Christmas week then stored on the back porch for the remainder of the year to collect dust and shrink in comparison to Angelica's body.

Learning to ride a bike, based on the human instruction manual that comes with each child, should be completed by age six. Angelica was close to eight before Aaron and I realized it was definitely time to give her private bike lessons. We wanted to ensure she had another outlet for good, enjoyable exercise.

My husband, the experienced rider in the family, took on the task of teaching Angelica. The first day focused on riding with the training wheels attached, as did the second and third days. By the fourth day, it was time to remove the wheels. The big moment had arrived. I imagined Angelica hopping onto the bike and pedaling enthusiastically into the sunset. As soon as she got on the bike, reality immediately tarnished my vision. Aaron initially used charm to encourage Angelica to get on the bike, continually communicating his confidence in his daughter's ability. Angelica was hesitant, concerned for her fragile knees. She worried that her

daddy, despite his reassurances, would not be there when she wobbled slightly, wobbled again, and then fell.

Their bike training ritual continued. Angelica would get on the
bike and insist that her father firmly hold the back of her padded,
pink seat for stabilization. He would hold the seat reassuringly; she
would pedal. He would let go; she would pedal. When she realized
her father's stabilization device (his hand only lighting touching
the seat) was missing, she would fall. Discussions between father
and daughter became heated. It was nearing the end of one of
their sessions and getting late. I went in the house and started preparing dinner. I was so absorbed in my activities, I forgot about the
momentous event outside.

Suddenly Angelica stomped into the house, tired and dejected.
She rushed passed me and into the bathroom. Soon I heard the
sound of the shower running over her body. Several minutes later,
my husband entered through the front door, laughing to himself.
Later I found out what had happened. It appeared Angelica was
minutes away from achieving the mission: learning to ride a bike
with confidence. Then she lost control of her front wheel. Before my
husband could grab her, Angelica moved rapidly toward a ditch—
a muddy ditch—and forgot all the lessons of the day (particularly
the need to brake). She was ejected, pink helmet first, bottom last.
When she recovered her composure and stood up, Angelica had
mud from head to toe. Yuk and double yuk! Then the ceremonious
march back to the house began, minus the bike and her father.

* * *

Angelica started karate when she was seven. My husband thought
it was an activity they would do together, something that would
bring countless hours of joy to their father-and-daughter relationship. Karate would also allow Angelica to get some needed exercise, learn to protect herself, and, if she achieved high levels of
performance, maybe even teach one day.

Angelica and Aaron picked a studio near our home and started classes. Angelica enjoyed taking the classes, and the demands for home practicing were less rigorous than those for piano. As a result of school conflicts, Aaron had to drop out within months, but he was convinced Angelica should continue her mastery. I had the dubious task of taking her to class twice a week, Friday nights and Saturday mornings. Unlike piano, despite her lethargic attitude, Angelica began to excel. One summer, her sensei recommended she participate in a local tournament. We hesitated. Angelica was a girl who had, at best, a lackadaisical attitude toward her craft. Her sensei thought the tournament would be a good motivator for someone with obvious talent but a sheer lack of desire. We were partly convinced. On the day of the tournament, we headed for the west side of Jacksonville and dropped Angelica off early so she could register and prepare for the contest.

Aaron and I have always been proud of Angelica. However, as we waited for the contest to start, we had mixed feelings. The katas for the various belts were to be performed first, starting with white belts and ending with black belts. Then the sparring would begin. Angelica was a greenbelt at the time. When she finally moved onto the mats, our spirits dropped as we saw her all-male, all-energetic challengers. The competitors performed the requested kata together, moving nimbly across the floor, almost like a single organism. They swished their bodies in unison, their feet gliding across the blue padded mats, their arms and hands making elegant movements in the cool air. I mainly watched Angelica although at times I took little peeks at her competition. I was proud of her. She projected complete peace and poise in what she was doing, and I was in a trance. My daze was broken as the competitive kata section ended. Angelica came running toward us, glad to have completed her kata without forgetting anything. As we waited for the results, we expected an honorable mention. However, her sensei was convinced we could expect much more. As the honorable mentions began and Angelica's name was not announced, Aaron and I looked at each other with slight bewilderment. Fourth place was not Angelica. Third place was not Angelica. We began thinking they had missed her from the list of contestants. We were so proud of our baby girl when she was awarded second place in her skill level. As a mother, I was proud at her accomplishment, and my satisfaction was magnified by the fact that she did it her way, with understated confidence and underlying natural talent!

Angelica continued to take karate at the same dojo on Friday nights and Saturday mornings for eight years. Her initial lack of desire slowly moved into apathy, her attendance primarily driven by my sense of obligation to the sensei, who had become a personal friend of Aaron's. By now, Angelica was a brown belt, and her younger brother, Aaron Kendrick IV, had arrived on the scene. In preparation for her black-belt certification, her sensei started to allow Angelica to teach classes, but even that was little motivation. So I stopped taking her. Her sensei called a few times, almost pleading for me to bring her back, promising that once she received her black belt everything would change. Angelica was happy. She was tired of the Friday-night and Saturday-morning ritual. I told the sensei Angelica would only be back if she asked to return. She never did.

Several years later, Angelica declared her frustration that after eight years of pushing her, I had let her quit karate when she was so close to her black-belt exam. I smiled. I wasn't falling for her emotional blackmail. "Well," I said, "if you ever want to start again, you know where the dojo is!" She stalked away. Maybe a sense of personal regret appeared on her face. Nevertheless, Angelica didn't have enough personal disappointment to go back to the dojo and complete her black-belt exam.

Chapter Four

"The phone took over Angelica's life."

Oh Boy, A Teenage Girl

I choose not to remember Angelica developing her sexuality as a teenager. I like to reflect on her as an asexual creature unaffected by the opposite sex. However, I remember Angelica developing her sexuality at a young age. I'd hoped the subject wouldn't come onto the scene again until after she reached her wedding day. I dreamed of spending precious moments with her before she spoke her vows. As she prepared to be a bride, I would discuss my first time making love. Well, the reality was a bit different.

Angelica's sexuality became apparent to me when she was about five. She liked to play with her vagina, unhindered by the neurosis of society's norms. Aaron and I ignored her natural desires to seek personal pleasure. Aaron? Well, I am not sure he realized what was going on. And me? I considered it a normal rite of passage and had flickering recollections back to my own child-hood. Angelica quickly learned that playing with her vagina was best performed in the privacy of her room. But we didn't make a big deal of the activity, and it didn't last long. And that's it. The topic of Angelica and sex was over (at least for the remainder of her childhood).

* * *

Angelica and I were inseparable when she was younger. We were mother and daughter. I instructed and she did. I chastised and she cried. I demanded and she cooperated. But things started to change as Angelica drifted into her teenage years. I told and she questioned. I chastised and she quizzed. I demanded and she resisted. Our lives became a series of arguments.

Looking back, those times often felt as if I were arguing with myself. Angelica's arguments felt familiar and comfortable to me. I felt the rightness of her protests; they had been right to me many years before. However, the rightness then came with consequences, consequences that were oftentimes painful and always somewhat distressing. They were consequences that I could see vividly as a mother but were not even vague thoughts when I'd been a teenager. My whole body and soul fought for my daughter, fighting for her not to experience the pains and challenges I'd had as a teenager, fighting for my baby girl not to grow up, struggling to ensure Angelica would learn from my lessons and not her own. Our mother-daughter relationship from birth became romanticized by me.

The changes in our relationship were contained within a series of events: first makeup, first diet, first "friend," first boyfriend, and senior year in high school. This series was balanced by a sequence of events into adulthood: Angelica's first real disappointment with a boy, her second disappointment with a boyfriend, an argument with her best friend, an argument with her new "life-long" best friend, and so on. Scattered between Angelica's disappointments were decision-making events that could have resulted in true set-backs in her life choices. However, things such as studying, taking the SAT, discussing a college major, and picking a college seemed relegated to secondary decisions in Angelica's life. After all, she had to worry about her ever-growing and increasingly complex social life.

Appearance Is Everything

Watching your daughter turn into an outwardly curvaceous woman is like watching an exotic butterfly's metamorphosis, although the metamorphosis is not quite as clear with teenagers. It's almost as if they drift between each of the stages: caterpillar…cocoon…butterfly…cocoon…caterpillar…butterfly. It was during this meandering that I realized Angelica was becoming a woman.

It was seventh grade picture time at school. Usually I received a little italicized note on bright paper, reminding me it was picture time. The note included a date, time, and a reminder to dress my child in her Sunday best. But this time I received no notes, no reminders. The first time I realized it was possibly picture day was when Angelica marched out of her room, ready for school with moments to spare. Her hair was immaculately combed, straight and dark with the slight trace of endless hours of brushing and grooming. Two pieces of hair dangled from each side of her forehead, and she wore blue dungarees with a matching top. This was not a new outfit, but it looked different that day. Was it the top? Was it the crisp ironing? There was also a slight difference in her face; it was glowing. Her lips were drenched in a shiny gloss. I smiled and mentally captured the moment. The butterfly in her magnificence was appearing, if only for a moment.

Communication Devices Are More Important Than Oxygen

As a professed introvert from England, the whole extroverted social scene of an American teenage girl was difficult for me to imagine. An American teenage girl's life, desires, and happiness seem to be driven by her social popularity. This popularity appears to translate into a sense of well-being and happiness and is as basic a need as food and water. Popularity is determined by the number of "right" people within your alliances. Of course, in the technological age in which Angelica became a teenager, there was a new way to measure that popularity: the number of arguments with parents about cell phones.

Before Angelica had a cell phone, she was attached to our home phone. We had the normal (at least for that time) American home phone devices. All of our landline phones were the same make and model. Aaron had bought them on sale, something like four for the price of one. They were all wall-mounted phones. We had one in the kitchen, one in the bathroom upstairs, one in the study, and one spare. What can I say? They were cheap, and we were sure they wouldn't last long. We also had a top-of-the-line wireless phone. It was sleek, compact, and black, with a built-in answering machine that included every service imaginable.

Angelica's relationship with those phones—especially the wireless—started during her early teenage years. The whole relationship was innocuous at first. In fact, I encouraged the affair and celebrated the rapport she developed with her circle of friends. I was relieved Angelica had been accepted in one of the right allegiances and delighted that she had a new hobby apart from watching television.

As Angelica entered her teenage years, both Aaron and I worked full-time. When we would arrive home to start our evening routine, the phone would always ring. After long days at work, the night was too short to be bothered with the inconvenience of sales calls which usually occurred during dinner.

We trained Angelica to answer the phone for us. Using our scripted questions, she was able to recognize a salesperson within moments. She would politely tell the salesperson we were not interested and *click*, the mildly irritating evening disturbance was over. Having Angelica deal with the phone calls was liberating for Aaron and me. No more listening to annoying, empty phone rings when we suspected the caller was a salesperson. No more needing to remove blank messages from our answering machine after a salesperson hung up without speaking. No more needing to politely, if not abruptly, tell a salesperson we were not interested.

For Angelica, the task was energizing. She had always rushed to pick up the ringing phone, just in case it was for her. Now she could take her time. No one else even attempted to answer the phone. She was the master. Or possibly the phone controlled her.

Aaron's and my lives initially became more pleasant in the evenings. Conversations were continuous, unbroken by either Angelica (who was on the phone) or sales calls. Life was good.

Then the phone took over Angelica's life. Talking on the phone became an obsessive, compulsive disease. The phone would ring, and she would jump up to answer. The phone wouldn't ring, and she would jump up to make a call. Even our wireless phone pleaded for a period of recovery as the batteries went dead regularly.

The wireless phone became Angelica's constant companion. If the phone was missing, we knew it would be snuggled in the middle of Angelica's sheets, still warm, waiting patiently for the next call.

About a dozen girls, all Angelica's age, were regular callers. All except one attended Angelica's school. Angelica talked to most of them at least once per day, sometimes in group conversations and sometimes individually. I would always try to keep the lines of conversation open between the two of us, using the calls to inquire,

"Who was on the phone? How were they?" Sometimes I would ask more specific questions, more intimate questions. I found it bizarre that Angelica could never answer (or chose not to answer) these more private questions about her friends. I started to wonder exactly what they talked about for hour after hour.

Angelica's phone compulsion started to exhibit new symptoms. Aaron and I would come home, and there would be ten or twelve messages on the answering machine. The first message would be a pause, silence, and a click. Next message: a pause, silence, and a click. Next message: a pause, silence, and a click. It became clear that most of these calls came from Angelica's friends. This almost daily burden of cleaning the answering machine became a drain on Aaron and me, so we stopped deleting the messages. The machine became full of uncleared clicks, until finally, no more messages could be recorded. What a relief. We had overcome another irritation.

For the next few weeks, the phone rarely rang. When it did, Aaron and I felt refreshed and prepared to tackle any teenage girl on the other line and possibly a couple of salespeople too. Aaron and I had made it into a game to see who could get to the phone before Angelica and embarrass both Angelica and her friend by asking silly questions. The game felt like we were recapturing our youth. The more we played the game, the more youthful we felt and the older and more irritated Angelica acted. The whole scenario was a reversal of roles between daughter and parents. Or possibly the onset of really early parental Alzheimer. Aaron and I were having plenty of fun, fun, and more fun. Then, one day, I grabbed the phone and there wasn't a sweet little girl on the other end asking for Angelica. There was a boy.

The voice was deep but polite, requesting to speak to Angelica. This boy (hopefully not a man) was asking to speak to my baby girl. After letting Angelica know who was on the phone, I was so shocked about the change in events that I could do nothing but hand her the phone. Angelica nonchalantly took the phone and seemed to care little about the male's call. I told Aaron, and he and I spent the next twenty minutes attempting to listen in to Angelica's side of the conversation while struggling to decide what the boy on the other end of the line was saying. The call finished, and Aaron and I took different approaches to learn more about this boy we hadn't even known existed thirty minutes earlier. I started bombarding Angelica with questions, but she offered no meaningful reply. Her father initiated a more indirect approach to interrogating his daughter, which proved equally futile. We knew nothing other than a boy had called our house.

With boys calling the house, answering the phone became even more amusing, particularly for Aaron, who would try to scare the deep-voiced boys with his deeper, more confident voice. But it never worked. The boys always called back. Sometimes Angelica's disinterest in these "salesmen" callers translated into a reluctance to talk. Aaron and I would become the puppets required to provide excuses about why Angelica couldn't, or more appropriately *wouldn't*, answer the phone.

Just when we got used to the new routine of our lives—the phone constantly ringing with calls from various girls and boys— even more symptoms of Angelica's phone compulsion arrived. Usually when the phone rang, it would result in echoes throughout the whole house, the three wall phones ringing with the same high pitch, alternating with the wireless phone and its slower, lower pitch. Even the sleeping would stir.

One day Aaron's sister questioned where he had been one night when she called. Why hadn't he answered the phone? "It could have been important," she said. Aaron was puzzled and started searching for answers. He didn't have to search far. One of the phone ringers upstairs was off. Aaron switched on the ringer, the question answered.

A couple of weeks later, Angelica called upstairs. It was a phone call for her father. Aaron once again wondered why he hadn't heard the ring but presumed Angelica had been on the phone. After a couple more of these strange episodes, Aaron stopped questioning why the phone no longer rang at certain times of night. Instead, he started investigating. It didn't take him long to realize Angelica was turning the wall phones' ringers off so we wouldn't hear the wireless phone ringing in her room late at night. Aaron chastised Angelica repeatedly about this, but the ringers would still mysteriously get turned off, and sometimes they were left off in the morning.

I would be standing in the kitchen and hear the phone upstairs ringing from a distance and realize the kitchen phone's ringer was off again.

One day the wireless phone stopped working. Angelica was outraged. Her secret, late night talking would now have to come to an end, though not as a result of her parents' demands.

Angelica started using the wall units. However, they were not conveniently placed for long discussions, so she would prop herself up on a stool or balance on the kitchen countertop. Although the process of talking was more inconvenient and the midnight talks were prevented, her daily conversations didn't seem to dwindle. We thought we were winning the battle, but we were not sure who we were kidding—our conversations on these precariously placed wall units were just as uncomfortable as Angelica's!

Then the age of cell phones arrived. We were able to resist for a while, but with the advent of "family plans" and phone allowances from work, it seemed ridiculous not to purchase a cell plan that would at least let us talk with each other for a minimal monthly fee. This was a big mistake. It was like giving a recuperating drug addict an endless supply of drugs and requesting that she use her willpower not to inhale them. Angelica was elated to receive her own, slightly bulky cell phone. We gave her a long list of sanctions:

The phone was only for emergencies. The phone could only be used in nonemergencies for Angelica to call us or for us to call her. Emergency numbers included aunties, uncles, and the police.

It took about three months before we received our first bill. The hours were reasonable, although heavily weighted toward Angelica. But we didn't go over our cell-plan minutes. Aaron merely noted that Angelica had used more phone hours than ours put together, but he said nothing.

Our next bill took another two months to arrive, and it was much larger than it should have been if we didn't go over our monthly minutes. Aaron audited the bill. Angelica had doubled the number of minutes she had used from the prior month. She also had large volumes of text messages to her friends each day. There were calls at midnight and in the early morning. Aaron, angry at the enormity of the bill, confronted Angelica; her reaction was calm and concise. The large bill was our fault. We had a bad plan not enough minutes, no endless text messaging, and no nights of free calling. Aaron, in as calm a voice as possible, reminded Angelica that the cell phones were only for emergencies, therefore a laundry list of special features would not be needed if the phones were only used for that purpose. It took a colossal bill of over a thousand dollars (five times greater than the basic service) for Angelica to get the message, but she finally did. Angelica's cell phone was removed for several weeks. It was like removing an addict's drugs.

Angelica's withdrawal was painful to everyone in the house. She would stomp around the house aimlessly, face contorted, shoulders hunched. Without the constant calling and text messaging, Angelica started to show positive signs that her addiction was being broken. She started engaging me in conversation again, fully participated in family activities without constantly looking at her phone, and laughed at her father's absurd jokes.

Once Angelica started college and began working part-time on campus, there was only one thing on her mind: getting her own phone plan. Of course she knew what each carrier offered and the plan she wanted. I believe her plan offered several thousand minutes; limitless text messaging; and free weekends, nights, and holidays. However, we were all happy. Angelica was paying her own phone bill and was glued to her cell phone with accompanying camera and other gadgets. We had a separate plan, with predictable, manageable costs. Aaron and I celebrated our newly found freedom with new, high-tech Motorola Razr phones. Even Angelica was impressed.

Vengeance shouldn't be sweet, but it is. One day Angelica either didn't think she needed to pay her whole bill or simply didn't have enough money to do so. That month she paid a partial payment, and almost immediately, her phone was turned off. She frantically called me at work from a phone at school, asking my executive administrative assistant to find me immediately. It was an emergency. When I heard Angelica's rationale for declaring a crisis, I was slightly irritated. However, I also felt sorry she had a dilemma. Angelica will always be my baby girl. I never wanted to see her upset, especially if it was within my power to remedy her concerns.

Angelica wanted me to ask her father if he would pay her balance so she could reconnect her service. That evening, in clear earshot of Angelica's room, I presented Angelica's request to Aaron. His reaction was a combination of elation and a desire for revenge due to previous, unsettled phone bills. There was no need to tell Angelica his answer. She stomped past us both, agitated. She could not understand the motives for her father's euphoria, but in time she would. Sometimes justice is sweet.

The War of the Chores

There are many wars being fought in the world at present. Wars against terrorism using sophisticated, intelligent bombs, the winner takes all. Wars based on words, requiring meticulous diplomatic negotiations. There's usually no winner, just hour after hour of compromise. Decade-long religious wars full of the piercing smell of death. There are usually no victors but plenty of losers.

Angelica and I have experienced many mother-daughter wars. Many of them have centered on cleaning…or what I would say is *not* cleaning.

I started Angelica off at a young age with chores. She naturally adapted to helping me. All she wanted in life was to "be like Mummy." She loved pretend cooking, imaginary shopping, fantasy washing, and make-believe cleaning. I could see the pride in her face and stature when I allowed her to help in my daily tasks. She loved polishing the best, spraying oceans of lemon Pledge on the dining room table, rubbing and rubbing until the table was perfectly smudge-free. Just when I would think she was done, she would add another lake-like layer of spray and start polishing the table again. Of course, the memories are overly partially sentimentalized. Maybe the table wasn't quite as streak-free as I fondly remember.

I do vaguely recollect Angelica didn't always want to move on to cleaning another piece of furniture, so it sometimes required negotiation and shrewd persuasion to get her to progress further. Then there was the time she used wood polish on glass. The result was not a pretty sight. But mainly the memories are good, mother and daughter cleaning together, bonding together, capturing moments Angelica would be able to pass on to her daughter.

As Angelica became older, she started resenting her chores. No longer did she attack them with a youthful glow and a child-like desire to imitate her mother. Instead, she took her antipathy out on her tasks. Talk shows on the topic of chores stated the inevitability that children would complete their chores at a barely passing grade. When I watched these shows, I knew it would be different with Angelica. I was always a meticulous child, and my room was always clean. I also made extra money cleaning my auntie's and nanny's house. I enjoyed cleaning all their cupboards, corners, and hard-to-reach areas. I knew I had introduced Angelica to cleaning at the correct age, which when mixed with a genetic predisposition for tidiness guaranteed results rather than conflict. But I was wrong. As Angelica grew older, a metaphorical, decade-long conflict began. This War of the Chores included all the signs of war figurative blood, death, and famine, mixed with literal anger and rage.

The decade-long War of the Chores began with rumors and rumblings of battle. Angelica had started to slack on her chores, and whenever I mentioned something to her that needed done, the result would be a stalemate. During these episodes we would invite others into the conflict such as my husband. Like a good neutral country, Aaron would not take sides. However, sometimes the chore crimes were just too monstrous for him to ignore. At those times he would move swiftly over to support the larger aggressor, which would be me, the mother country.

The greatest wars were fought over Angelica's room. Usually Angelica's other chores around the house would still be done, either late or incomplete, but her room existed in a totally different universe. Just like hotdogs, a teenager's messy room is an American institution. However, during our decade-long war Angelica took a dirty room to a whole new level. At first I would demand the room be cleaned once a week, sheets included. However, week after week the demand became less effective and more draining. So I just stopped requesting and eliminated Angelica's room from my purview. I pretended we just had three bedrooms rather than four. My mind game worked best if I kept her door closed, and Angelica cooperated when she left her room or the house, her bedroom door would be closed.

Of course, there were times when Aaron stumbled upon the extra room and demanded its cleaning. He would wander around the outward expression of teenage resistance and discover mounds of discarded paper under the bed, shoes and clothes from prior months' outfits on the floor, half-eaten dinners from the previous week, dog vomit hardened on the carpet, and the accumulated remains of daily makeup and hair rituals abandoned on Angelica's dressing-room table. Aaron would usually leave the room in complete disbelief that someone actually lived there. To make matters worse, Angelica didn't seem to mind. Oftentimes she invited her friends to enter this disaster area, exhibiting no concern about the debacle called her bedroom. I would often query her friends on their reaction to the calamity Angelica called her room. They would grin mischievously and usually declare their rooms were worse!

Of course, as I became a little more experienced and wiser, I tried negotiation tactics: bribing, enticing, and persuading were all parts of my armory. I even tried cleaning Angelica's room from top to bottom until it was spick and span. Although I must admit I had a bit of an ulterior motive during those episodes. After watching talk shows that almost demanded you examine your teenager's room on a frequent basis, I decided I would attempt to see what I could find. However, I didn't know where to start. Also, I began feeling guilty about intruding into Angelica's personal space. I would discharge my remorse by thoroughly cleaning the bedroom from top to bottom.

I found nothing during these precarious adventures other than a fancy pair of thongs. Since I hadn't known that Angelica was wearing those uncomfortable fashion fiascos, my discovery was quite shocking.

Angelica was always pleased at my attempts to clean. Her pleasure would be followed by a series of commitments to maintain this new level of bedroom cleanliness. However, those commitments would be followed by her room slipping slowly into the same state of filthiness from whence it had come. I am told that as Angelica moves into her own place, her desire to take care of her possessions will change. Time will tell.

Let the Wallets Be Opened

Having lived in America for over fifteen years, marrying an American citizen, birthing three beautiful American-born children, and pledging my citizenship to America, I believed (possibly erroneously) that I was equipped to embrace all facets of American culture. I was wrong. I didn't realize how flawed my logic was until I collided with junior and senior year at an American high school.

Senior year was most shocking to my non-Americanized system. Of course I can't say I hadn't received warnings about this potential clash of cultures during Angelica's eighth-grade formal dance and her junior prom. In fact, the never-ending parade of American teenage movies spelled out what should be expected. However, these were movies, Hollywood's glamorization of the "real world." Weren't they?

The eighth-grade formal dance was my initial introduction into what was approaching. Angelica had been talking about the dance since the beginning of the school year. I don't remember having an initial thought when Angelica started talking about the event. I had no reference and no vision because I had never experienced a similar event when I had been in school. I was stepping in unfamiliar territory. In fact, I had never owned or even rented a long formal dress. I requested my daughter's guidance as I stumbled almost blindly down this unfamiliar road. Angelica, of course, could have led me astray. She could have led me into countless, expensive, loan-requiring stores. She didn't. Angelica could have taken advantage of me, but she didn't.

I was on my way to Atlanta on business around the same time Angelica was supposed to pick a dress, so we took the trip together. At the time this decision seemed innocuous. In years to come I realized it gave Angelica bragging rights related to the authenticity of her dress, it came from *Atlanta*. In American high school terms, the dress was categorized the same as a Paris original gown flown in from France that morning. I am sure the story was enhanced further, possibly with the dress being identified as a one-of-a-kind garment made especially for Angelica by a world-renowned, Atlanta-based designer.

The whole process of picking the eighth-grade formal dress wasn't as confrontational as I expected. Angelica was only thirteen. Neither of us knew quite what to expect as we began our joint dress-buying adventure. I was unsure of whether Angelica wanted her dependence, independence, or interdependence at any given moment. Usually she jumped between complete reliance on me to an all-consuming desire for self-determination and autonomy in all decision-making. These mood swings contrasted with my desire to stop my baby girl from maturing into a fully independent woman. I desperately wanted to help her avoid some of the harsh lessons I had stumbled upon as I moved into adulthood.

As Angelica hit her teenage years, her general rejection of clothes I picked was one of the most painful lessons I learned. As Angelica had grown, I took pride in the fact she had my sense of style—creating outfits that were cute but multifunctional. Angelica enjoyed my taste in clothing as much as I adored dressing her. She would usually beam as a passerby commented on her latest matching hat or coordinating shoes. However, things were changing, and I was starting to learn the agonizing lesson that Angelica was not always interested in my impeccably planned outfits, especially if they came from Kmart.

I was concerned we would not be able to decide on a dress that met both our tastes, because I was unsure about how far I should support Angelica's desire to flaunt her body's newfound curves. I was concerned my self-effacing sense of style would stifle Angelica's growing sense of self-assured poise. I could tell by Angelica's cautious approach to our shopping expedition that her emotions were similar.

Angelica had already tried on three or four outfits, all picked out by me. Most of them just didn't fit the newly defined curves of a thirteen-year-old. The air between us was a little caustic but manageable. It was the mission that was most important, not our sarcastic backbiting. Then suddenly, just like in a movie, we both saw a dress we thought was perfect. It was black and made with figure-hugging fabric. The dress had no sleeves, and a high neckline contrasted with a low (but not too-low) plunging back. The most attractive part of the dress was a white scarf that trimmed the neck and backline then cascaded and merged into a beautiful trail in the back. I quickly looked through the sizes. Bingo. They had Angelica's size. She went to try on the dress.

I could hardly wait for Angelica to appear from the dressing room. When she reappeared, she looked beautiful. Of course, we would need to purchase the correct combination of undergarment paraphernalia, but even without those additions, the outfit looked stunning. When Angelica and I returned from Atlanta, we both felt quite accomplished. We had found a dress and managed to do so together.

When Angelica prepared to leave for the formal dance a few weeks later, I hovered around her, providing assistance only when requested. Her makeup, her hair, and zipping the dress were all my responsibilities. Then she was done. Angelica glided out to show her father her newly found elegance. Aaron was stunned but held in his pleasure, preferring to taunt his baby girl. After a final parade and words of warning, Aaron and I took Angelica to the dance.

As we neared the dance, my heart pounded faster. The precious moment seemed more like my own than my daughter's. I noticed a rainbow of girls in beautiful dresses, laughing, joking, and running. There was something so special about watching the young people arrive in their beautiful gowns and handsome suits. Their gowns represented future goals, hopes, and dreams, unjaded by the realities of life. I watched as doting parents kissed their babies goodnight, initiating the process of releasing their children into semi-adulthood. I watched as chaperones shuffled those objects of hope into the ballroom. At first glance, the girls looked like women, at second glance like chuckling girls, giggling with their friends, accepting their newfound beauty. The young men stood like magnificent lions (lions waiting to attack their prey).

Angelica stepped out of our car with her stunning gown. Her hair was in an elaborate bun. Her nails were manicured to perfection and she had a slight touch of makeup on her face. All I could see was my baby girl dressed up in so many Easter Sunday dresses of the past. Her outward appearance was a mixture of adult sophistication and childhood innocence. I watched as she maneuvered her way to her friends, who were all giggling, chatting, and waving excitedly. I also felt every young male lion being drawn to the beauty of my daughter. They stood a little taller and appeared slightly more stylish as she passed. I felt uneasy, but Aaron restarted the car and drove slowly away, maneuvering through a crowd of cars and figures. Then the discomforting moment was over, and the scene faded.

* * *

Fortunately, after the eighth-grade formal I had three years to recuperate before the next milestone in high school partying arrived, and it appeared with a bang. It was the eleventh-grade prom; the event was a dress rehearsal for the senior prom. However, unlike most dress rehearsals, the clothes were expected to be new, stunning, and expensive. Angelica had moved out of her dependent-teenager phase. She expected to be treated like an independent adult, minus the wherewithal, worldly view of life, or a job to sustain a certain lifestyle. We were able to argue about the prom dress Angelica would wear and I would purchase. We generally argued about most things, and a junior prom dress provided the perfect opportunity to exercise our power.

I had already decided I wasn't about to waste my whole afternoon for an unappreciative teenage girl. I definitely wasn't going to waste my money on a dress that was not respectable. Angelica, based on her overall appearance, had decided she would put on her "Mummy dearest" act, presuming the pretense was necessary to extort the very dress she wanted, whatever the cost.

We returned to the same store at which we'd found Angelica's eight-grade formal gown: JCPenney. But this time the store was in Jacksonville rather than Atlanta. Angelica definitely took more of a leading role. She had spent several years fine-tuning her shopping skills, and she knew just what she liked and where to seek the ideal outfit. She was also willing to browse in several stores and try on several dresses before choosing the perfect match. The whole outing felt daunting, but I was trying to remain calm and composed, regardless of the emotional and financial costs.

We ended up visiting three stores, all in the same mall and situated close to each other. The final dress of choice was chosen by Angelica; surprisingly the experience was very similar to what had happened with her eighth-grade dress. We both immediately fell in love with the same dress. It was dark brown with gold embroidery, strapless, and had corset-like crisscross lacing in the back. It fit perfectly. To celebrate our single-minded accomplishment we purchased matching jewelry and the appropriate undergarments to flawlessly complement the dress.

The night of the prom was very similar to the eighth-grade formal. However, this time I didn't hover around Angelica as she had her hair, nails, and makeup professionally completed. That evening as Aaron waited to take Angelica to the prom, our house was full of a combination of excitement and trepidation. Boys had now entered into the picture, and the thought of releasing Angelica, even for a few hours, into a group of testosterone-filled boys was daunting. I took the obligatory pictures then released my daughter to ride with her father to the school gym for the prom. Afterward she was picked up promptly at midnight.

When I got the pictures developed, although the body was a graceful, elegant woman's, it was so comforting for me to still see my baby girl's chubby cheeks smiling back at me.

Before I knew it, senior year arrived. As usual, it had slipped into my life uninvited in many ways, while in other ways I had anticipated it for a lifetime. I expected Angelica to spend the year in serious studying and focusing on future prospects. Instead, her year was identified by a set of predetermined events in preparation for the senior prom.

It started with the senior yearbook deposit. The book cost so much money it was recommended parents pay for it in three easy installments. This was the book that would capture all the memories of Angelica's senior year. The deposit was a guarantee of reserving a book that would be sold with no money-back guarantee of satisfaction. Angelica was frantic in her demands for the deposit funds. She seemed convinced without this book of memories, all her high school memories would be lost in the wind of the next tropical storm.

I pondered her obsession for a moment. I was unsure why she wanted to capture such a group of confusing memories—memories of lifetime hurts, painful first loves lost, and girlfriends who became enemies. In many ways, Angelica's final two years of high school paralleled an afternoon soup opera rather than a serious environment of learning. And now I was expected to deposit large sums of money to capture those once painful but now romanticized moments!

Next, it was time for picture deposits for extremely classy glamour shots. The large initial sitting fee was only a prelude to the actual price of the prints. The pictures were taken in the atmosphere of a sophisticated Hollywood studio. Each "model" was encouraged to take her pictures both alone and with a parade of her very best friends. Shortly after taking the pictures, Angelica received an upscale, packaged set of irresistible proofs with a large ransom price attached. Of course, I was obligated to buy large numbers of these pictures, if not as a result of my own desires, then definitely as a product of my daughter's brainwashing. It was clear to me after several days of badgering that only an irresponsible, negligent parent would resist such an amazing opportunity to capture a daughter in such elegant poses. I started to seriously consider taking out a large loan in order to afford the remainder of Angelica's senior year.

Shortly after the pictures came the high school homecoming, followed quickly by the senior dance. At that point I was just relieved Angelica was driving and able to pick a dress without requesting large amounts of time from me. The senior dance proved to be the final hiatus prior to a frantic spending spree leading up to the senior prom. There were monies requested for graduation announcements that were akin in sophistication, design, and cost to wedding invitations. There were monies needed for pictures of Angelica in graduation regalia that were for insertion into the invitations. There were monies for a senior ring Angelica thought was second-rate, while I was certain it was superior to my wedding ring in elegance and cost. At the point where the momentous demands for money grew numbing, preparations for the prom arrived.

Angelica definitely showed glimmers of maturing into a responsible adult. As she talked about dresses for weeks with both her friends and me, she also discussed and acknowledged her budget constraints. Fortunately her many adventures to posh clothing establishments did not require my presence. Then one day she came home, excited, insisting she had found *the* dress she wanted to wear to the prom. That weekend, with a newly found sense of liberation, I willingly accompanied Angelica to visit *the* dress. Unlike prior dresses, the dress was definitely a little more sophisticated and revealing in all the wrong places. However, the dress was very complementary of Angelica's well-matured feminine attributes. It was respectfully low in both the front and the back and was a stunning turquoise color that truly complemented Angelica's skin. The matching undergarments were daintier and feminine, in contrast to the heavier, corset-like, claustrophobic undergarments of prior years. We also splurged and purchased matching shoes, a handbag, and dress jewelry. Oh yes, and there was the after-the-dance outfit too!

The afternoon and evening of the prom was something I could only compare to a prelude to a wedding. There was a hairdresser appointment, a manicure and pedicure, and even a professional makeup artist assigned to the event. At times I pinched myself as proof it was not my daughter's bridal day! At the end of endless hours of preparation, Angelica, with a sophisticated but girlish charm, was ready to leave. Since Angelica was not ready on time, she was fortunate that her date was respectfully late. They missed their dinner reservation, but no one was hungry anyway. We took endless rolls of pictures then accompanied the couple to their day-rental SUV.

I was both excited and saddened by the whole event. It was a moment we had been building up to for years, but in many ways, it felt empty and superficial to me, not something that I really wanted to support or celebrate. However, I desperately tried. The prom was the American Way. I just hoped and prayed my daughter would grow out of such shallow events and start to yearn for more insightful pastimes. I knew in time her desires would change, but since the prom was important for Angelica, I felt it was also important for me to share the memory making moment.

More Clothes, More Makeup, More Nail Styles: Time for a Part-Time Job

There always seems to be an absolute certainty about teenage sons starting work as soon as possible. It's almost as if their fifteenth birthdays are accompanied by demands they start work, the harder and tougher the job, the better. This expectation comes mostly from fathers for whom sons having jobs is a part of a boy's passage into manhood. Male adulthood requires a willingness and desire to work. When it comes to mothers and daughters, the requirement for work becomes more blurred. There appears to be a lack of motherly instinct requiring daughters to work as part of the passage into motherhood. The necessity for work appears attached to the requirement that girls remain fashionable with both their friendly and unfriendly competition, which some would call "girlfriends."

Angelica's first job was volunteering as part of a requirement for her college scholarship. Angelica and I agreed, or possibly I recommended and Angelica relented, she would volunteer at the local not-for-profit hospital. I clearly remember the day of orientation. Angelica was fourteen years old and she was well into her rebellious years, although I continued to fight to maintain the prior order of our mother-daughter relationship. I sought the order of when I said and she did, when I recommended and she agreed, and when I dreamed of her future and she approved of my dreams.

Even though Angelica was deep into a seditious phase, she was wise enough to realize her continued dependence on her father and mother. So with a blasé, compliant attitude, she sat in my car waiting for us to arrive at the hospital for volunteer orientation. Of course I was bubbling with excitement. Volunteering was part of my vision for my daughter. The work would be an excellent addition to Angelica's résumé. I was bubbling and babbling, demanding the same sense of enthusiasm from my daughter. I kept talking to Angelica about how the six-week excursion would shape college decisions many years down the road, how volunteering at the hospital could help to differentiate her college application from others. Every now and again I peeked over at Angelica; she appeared listless, living in some sort of parallel, less-exciting universe where my gibberish was incomprehensible.

Finally we arrived and maneuvered our way through the maze of indistinguishable corridors and floors to the hospital's volunteer orientation room. Throughout the search for the right floor and the correct room, I continued my excited babbling. Angelica remained a few steps behind me in a hesitant, disassociated teenage droop. When we turned the corner to the correct corridor and the volunteer-receiving room, we were welcomed by several adult volunteer coordinators. They shared or possibly surpassed my own level of excitement. They started to ask Angelica a series of questions. All the questions took several minutes for translation into the language of Angelica's parallel universe. Then she would answer in a quiet, concise manner: "Yes, ma'am. No, ma'am." When the answers appeared incomplete or distant, I (as any good translator would) added additional interpretation to ensure the correct level of excitement and commitment was received by the questioners. After a long period of questioning, Angelica and I were released to enter a large holding room. As I looked around the room, I was slightly surprised to see the endless sea of teenagers with one or sometimes both parents present. Most of the teenagers brought the same apathy as Angelica. Of course, there were also those bothersome exceptions to the rule, teenagers who transcended Angelica's parallel universe. Those teenagers appeared happy to be attending the orientation. They clearly understood the important role the volunteering might play in their college choices.

As the orientation began, the Director of Hospital Volunteer Services welcomed us and asked for all students to move forward.

The teenagers began disengaging themselves from their devoted parents and moved closer to the front. My automatic response was to hold Angelica tightly, concerned that without my puppeteer skills she would not respond correctly to the next phase of the interview. Then we would be unable to continue the orientation. Of course not continuing had unheard of ramifications. Angelica would not be accepted into the college of my...I mean *her* dreams. Looking back at the feelings of that moment, they were intense, absolute in their power to distort emotions. My response was an emotion to protect and nurture my child whatever the cost. Many parents around me had similar thoughts and emotions, but finally, with the coaxing of the director, all the candidates moved to the front.

The orientation began. The director reiterated the importance of volunteering, discussing the successes of prior students involved in the program and discussing the rules, schedules, and possible areas requiring volunteers. As I listened, my eyes got wider and wider. The program was more than I ever imagined. It was incredible. It was fantastic. It was perfect. What an opportunity!

The director started asking questions, and four or five potential volunteers' hands shot up. I could have identified the hand-raisers ahead of time. All of the parents could have picked these adolescents beforehand. At this point, the nonparticipating teenagers' parents bonded into a protective body. We had each been taking note of these strange, hand-raising teenagers' actions. Their enthusiasm and their devoted parents became the collective enemy because the parents of these children represented everything we hadn't been able to accomplish as parents. Their teenagers were responsive, participative, and obedient, and they lived their parents' dreams. When these teenagers were chosen to answer questions, the answers were always eloquent and complete. It was as if their parents were answering for them. The "other" group of parents sat on the sidelines, willing their teenagers to raise their hands, and I was no different. I knew Angelica could have answered each question. Based on her life experiences, I was sure some of Angelica's responses would be just as passionate as the answers we were hearing. As each question was asked, Angelica's possible answers kept playing through my head.

"Why are you here?"

"I love working with children," Angelica might say. "I have two baby brothers, and I enjoy helping my mother take care of them."

"Why did you choose this hospital?"

"Because it supports the poor and impoverished, the people most in need of care."

Just as other parents did with their children, I tried to get Angelica's attention. But her gaze was locked, staring beyond the director. She was mesmerized by the happenings of her alternate universe, barely comprehending the jabbering around her.

Before long, the orientation was over. Angelica was given her orientation package and told to expect further details of where her reporting assignment would be in a couple of weeks.

Angelica ended up being assigned to the labor and delivery group. This was my first choice (she had shrugged when asked her preference at the orientation, so I had provided an answer). The program lasted eight weeks. After the first day, Angelica showed the first signs of excitement. Her supervisor was obviously very encouraging. Angelica had exceeded expectations on day one by categorizing, organizing, and filing in her supervisor's office. On day two, Angelica was slightly bored her supervisor was in an all-day meeting. Without the close supervision, direction, and nurturing she received the day before, Angelica appeared frustrated with the lack of tasks to complete. On day three, Angelica's supervisor described her role at the hospital—she was a nurse midwife. She also discussed her educational path with Angelica. On day four, Angelica was invited to attend a birth but declined.

Declined? I wondered when I found out. *Why?*

Within a week Angelica was settling into the day-to-day routine of the hospital. She became familiar with the protocol of the unit where she worked and felt comfortable coordinating her daily and weekly tasks.

Of course for Angelica, avoiding additional opportunities to watch live births remained of utmost importance. Since she was in a labor and delivery ward, circumventing those harrowing events was virtually a full-time job.

Angelica was most adept at listening to the gossip-mill of the hospital. She knew all the latest stories of who was doing what to whom. Some of her stories were quite contagious, and oftentimes I couldn't wait to pick her up and hear the latest episode of an unfolding tale.

There was the ten-year-old girl who had had triplets. Although this horrifying story saddened me, I was comforted that Angelica had learned some difficult life truths. She was a little older and wiser after providing the final update of the saga.

Then there was the tale of the mother who had had her baby prematurely. After the baby had been in the hospital for many weeks, it was time for the mother to take her child home. In most people's lives this would be a time of preparation and excitement, however, not in this case. Angelica was shocked to tell me the mother didn't pick up her child as expected. If the mother didn't pick up her child the next day, the child would be considered abandoned then released to the state. As Angelica told the story, I could once again see she looked a little more mature. I didn't rejoice in others' pain but was grateful to see the positive impact these events had on my daughter's life.

Angelica volunteered at the hospital for two years, once in labor and delivery and once in the Neonatal Intensive Care Unit (NICU). I had my qualms when she chose the NICU her second year. I wanted to protect Angelica from the unthinkable sorrow that is part and parcel of the NICU. However, I soon realized that with much pain comes much pleasure and gain. Although it came with heartache, the joy Angelica brought home from her summer in the NICU will live with each of us for many years to come.

Before her senior year, Angelica made it clear that volunteering was out of the question; she was looking for a paid position. I hesitated, knowing in the long run her experiences at the hospital would be equally rewarding. However, Angelica was a full-fledged teenager by this time, and her ballooning expenses definitely deserved a summer position. She ended up being offered a position at a local law firm.

I thought this diversity of work experience would help Angelica decide on a career major for college. I was excited about the opportunity. I spent the night before Angelica's first day of work educating her on the etiquette of working in an office environment. Angelica educated me on how to roll your eyes and portray a complete disinterest in anything your mother communicates. I persisted: Do arrive on time and ready to work. Do smile and greet all adults. Do use polite phrases such as "yes, ma'am" and "no, ma'am." Don't leave early or arrive late from lunch. Don't call friends when you have nothing else to do. And above all else, don't wear any inappropriate clothing.

The mention of clothes thrust Angelica back into the conversation. Her eyes stopped rolling, her stance erected, and she started looking directly in my eyes. Initially I was caught off guard by this sudden interest in my one-way conversation. Then a warm feeling of motherhood started running through my body. I missed what Angelica said, but her face looked expectantly for a reply. It was almost as if we were sitting in separate cosmos again and communication between us took a couple of light-years to receive and decode. Then I realized what Angelica said. She had zeroed in on the clothes discussion and determined she had nothing appropriate to wear for work.

I came crashing down to reality but managed to remind myself I was the adult. My response needed to be appropriate to my role. I spent moments determining an appropriate reaction. I thought about pulling all the inappropriate clothes out of Angelica's wardrobe and throwing them in the trash, making it easy to pinpoint appropriate outfits. I pondered for a moment then realized this was probably not an appropriate reaction. I considered screaming at the top of my voice, rambling about how many sacrifices I had made over the years and how unappreciative Angelica appeared. Of course, I would also have to throw in the occasional example of children starving in the world. Again, probably not an appropriate response. I thought about putting my hands around Angelica's neck and choking her to death, hoping and praying that my next child would be a girl. This would allow me to use my prior experiences to bring up a more appreciative young lady. Unfortunately this last idea was not only an inappropriate reaction but would result in a lengthy incarceration.

While dismissing each of these thoughts, I slowly pulled myself into a standing position, conscious that at any moment I could snap and not remember anything until I woke up in jail. I cautiously maneuvered over to the closet bulging with clothes, mindful that I came from a line of African royalty that required dignified behavior in all circumstances. I positioned myself next to the altar of clothes, elevating my posture into a dignified masquerade suited to a princess. Within moments, I started to plan a business wardrobe for the next week. Once I had a certain level of agreement from Angelica, I whisked myself out of her room before something inappropriate happened. Weeks later I bought Angelica three new outfits on sale since she had performed her law clerk position flawlessly to that point. (At least that's what I like to imagine.)

Danger: Teenager Driving

There are many cultural differences between England and the United States, and many of the disparities appear during the teenage years. Driving and having a car is a right of passage with teenagers in the United States. In England, none of my friends drove cars. None of my younger cousins are presently learning how to drive. I can't remember any friends driving themselves to sixth form (the equivalent of eleventh and twelfth grades in high school). When I went to school, learning to drive wasn't even something we discussed, but there appear to be three very important teenage milestones in the States. No, not picking your high school, getting into college, and selecting a major. But rather receiving your learner's permit before your friends, accomplishing the feat of passing your final driver's test, and finally getting the type of car you want. Preferably the car will be new and coincide with a teenager's sixteenth birthday.

Angelica started to prepare me for these rights of passage at an early age. By the time she reached middle school, she started to question her father and me on the specifics of when she should plan on getting her driver's license. She preceded these questions with a comprehensive education to both of us on when she could get her learner's permit and, more importantly, what the minimal requirements were for moving from the learner's permit to being able to take the test for a Florida driver's license. The whole discussion might as well have been gibberish to me. I had no point of reference for the etiquette of when a teenager should begin the process of learning how to drive. Fortunately, Angelica's father, a Florida native, had plenty of experience. With Aaron's knowledge we developed a plan. Angelica would call it a plan of humiliation. Her parents would call it a sensible plan of preparation.

The thought of Angelica driving made me very nervous; it made me drift back to my first precarious lessons. My initial introductory driving lessons were not like most American children, propped on my father's lap in the driver's seat at the age of four. Instead, my initial lesson came at the ripe old age of twenty. Rather than begging to learn to drive, I was a reluctant participant. My father-in-law was the first person who alluded to the possibility it was time for me to drive. I had been in the United States for sixth months, using the snail-like city bus system to transport me from one side of the city to another. My father-in-law coaxed me to get into the driver's seat of his car. It was time for my first lesson.

I had never been in the driver's seat of a car before. I could also count on both hands the times I sat in the three passengers' seats of any car before I moved to America. As my father-in-law opened the driver's door and I timidly slid behind the steering wheel, a sense of trepidation began to rise from my feet to my legs, up through my stomach, and finally to my arms and the tips of my fingers. Small beads of sweat appeared on my brow. My nerves made me feel like I was walking through an old cemetery on a Halloween night with a full moon. Every motion my father-in-law made resulted in small, involuntary jumps of my heart, which was now positioned in my mouth. My lack of familiarity with the workings of a car meant it took thirty minutes for me to understand how the fuel and gas pedals worked, forget the other vehicular intricacies. By the time the car was started, I had forgotten the first thirty minutes of lessons. The ten-minute drive around the block resulted in a scary-movie mixture of emotions ranging from spine-chilling to bloodcurdling. By the time we reached my father-in-law's house again, sweat ran down my forehead, and a band of water saturated the collar of my lilac, short-sleeved top.

Aaron had decided Angelica's first driving lesson would be on the way home from church. As Angelica maneuvered into the driver's seat for her first lesson, the memories of my own perilous driving reentered my head. I prepared for a frightening experience.

Aaron, Angelica, our two boys, and I all sat in the car for Angelica's first driving lesson. If the chapter ended badly, our little family would cease to exist. Angelica was comfortably positioned in the driver's seat. Our youngest child, Joshua, snoozed contentedly in his car seat. Our middle child, Aaron IV, protested and pleaded with his father to deposit him safely home before the lesson began. I was sandwiched between my sons. Aaron sat peacefully in the front passenger's seat, exhibiting a certain degree of pride and satisfaction. He prepared to pass on one of his happiest childhood memories: learning to drive with his father. Now we would teach his baby girl. On the other hand, I had my own less than satisfactory recollections of learning how to drive. I tried to remain calm, but I felt a sense of foreboding as Aaron IV persisted in verbalizing my worst-case crash fears.

The basic driving lessons continued for a number of weeks. Aaron IV and I felt like we were in each of the lessons, although most were actually taken only with father and daughter. Within a few months, Aaron felt Angelica was ready to start driving to school. Knowing Angelica was no longer a true beginning driver didn't make my anxieties vanish. Knowing there was a long, accident-prone expressway between home and school made my apprehension even worse. Knowing I was the chosen parent who would guide Angelica through her endless hours of practice on the accident-prone road made my stomach automatically cramp into what felt like a large baseball. However, as an obedient wife and encouraging mother, my excuses ran out. It was time to get down to the job of supporting my daughter's driving lessons in my two-year-new Jaguar.

My experiences with Angelica in a car remain consistent to this day. Our conversations were based on my role as a teacher and Angelica's role as a student. Sometimes our dialogues focused on my role as a protective mother and Angelica's role as a freedom-seeking daughter. When Angelica steps into the driver's seat, I still envision her sitting behind the wheel during her first driving lesson. Sometimes I even recall her taking her first steps. She's innocent, requiring my guidance and protection. Angelica, in turn, portrays a sense of individuality and independence, not needing help (particularly her mother's) to drive successfully from one location to another.

Angelica began practicing to drive each weekday on the way to school. Each morning, Angelica would move to the car at a snail's pace. Was her slow rate the result of a union-planned adolescent slowdown in reaction to unsatisfactory parenting conditions? As she slithered leisurely to the car, I would anticipate how many minutes late I would be to work if Angelica didn't hurry up. Her unhurried pace was both deliberate and purposefully measured. Looking back, her desire to irritate her mother and teacher before the driving lesson began was puzzling. Why would the pupil deliberately annoy her teacher? Why would the novice infuriate the instructor who had the power to deliver the freedom of knowledge?

Once we finally made it to our respective seats in the car, the lesson would begin. The tutorial always began the same way, with me asking (and sometimes answering) questions. Is the seat correctly positioned? Did you check your mirrors? Can you see correctly through them? Is your seatbelt on and loosely fitting? As the days, weeks, and months passed, Angelica provided the answers before I could safely buckle into my seat. As the mature adult, I would acknowledge my love for Angelica with a smile of purposed peace, and within moments we would be out on the road. The fifteen-minute drive through commuter traffic would be complemented by the sounds of my instruction: "Stop…Slow down…Use your indicator…Don't forget to look…Stop…Slow down…Use your indicator…Don't forget to look…Did you see that car? Stoooppp!"

There would be only a grunt of acknowledgement from the driver's seat. Other than these grunts, there was silence in the car, a mother and daughter sharing everything and nothing at the same time.

Upon arrival at Stanton College Preparatory High School, Angelica would generally park haphazardly in the parking lot. She usually took up two parking places or found some way to restrict all movement of traffic. She would jump out of the car, leaving the driver's door open as if relinquishing ownership of the two-year, nearly new Jaguar until after school. As I started toward the driver's seat, I would take the opportunity to use analogies to magnify the impact of Angelica's nonchalant parking. She would nod obediently as she grabbed her backpack from the trunk.

Angelica's countenance always changed from forbearance and restraint to charm and appeal as soon as she stepped away from the apparently depressive aura of the car and my pesky voice. As she approached the school, her pace changed from that of a slithering slug to an exquisite cheetah prowling through the crowd. She commanded attention from all the male beasts...I mean fellow studious students.

As the months passed in our driving lessons, the only thing that didn't remain the same was Angelica's appearance. As our driving lessons began, her slightly pudgy frame timidly maneuvered into school. As time continued, her frame became more curvaceous in all the right (or as a mother would say, *wrong*) places. By the time our driving lessons ended, she owned the path between the sidewalk and the entrance to the school. Angelica would acknowledge friends, laughing, joking, and smiling confidently. I relished each of these moments, treasuring the images of my daughter leaving the safety of my company. I stored the memories for a future when Angelica would need these flashes as I counseled her on her own teenage daughter. Or for when I would need them for moments of personal recollection and reminiscence.

From receiving a learner's permit to taking the final driving test should take at least one year. Angelica had a January birthday, so from the prior August to the beginning of the calendar year, many of Angelica's friends and colleagues received *their* licenses (or in some instances, were humiliated as they were unable to pass their final tests). Angelica, akin to a preeminent lawyer, used all of these testimonies in her argument to take the test as soon as the one-year mark of her driving had been reached. The scene was set as she created a story painted in parental guilt and shaded with parental responsibility and culpability. Within moments of Angelica meeting her one-year practice requirements, she presented her closing arguments. Within hours, she realized her father was unwilling to provide a specific date when she could take her test. Angelica was furious. She pleaded with Aaron, repeating previous arguments. She promised better school grades. She stalked around the house, silent and unresponsive. She failed to realize that her responses, as well as her less-than-satisfactory driving skills, had played into Aaron's decision—she was not ready for the freedom involved in being able to drive. Weeks passed and Angelica kept querying her father about getting her driver's license. His answer stayed the same. Then months passed and Aaron finally agreed Angelica was ready to take "The Test."

We agreed I would take Angelica to the Florida Department of Highway Safety and Motor Vehicles office closest to our house. I asked Angelica to setup the appointment, an early morning Friday appointment if possible. The next Friday morning, we were one of the first customers in line as the office opened at seven thirty. I was a little nervous Angelica would not pass and worried about the subsequent impact on her ever-changing mood. Angelica, in turn, looked excited and confident she would pass this "test for freedom" with flying colors.

We sat and waited. I desperately hoped the moment toward adulthood would never come, whereas Angelica willed the moment to pass successfully so she would gain the freedom to drive. Since this was the time before smart phones helped to cover awkward silences, we sat quietly, waiting and observing our surroundings.

Once Angelica's name was called, everything happened quickly. Angelica eagerly escorted the examiner to the then three-year-new Jaguar. The instructor appeared impressed at the sight of the car, and I wondered what varieties of vehicles were usually involved in teenagers' driving tests. Obviously, at least on this side of town, not Jaguars, even relatively inexpensive models. My mind started to wander as my car disappeared across the parking lot and into the adjacent neighborhood. Would the examiner be so impressed with the car she would pass Angelica even though she was not truly ready to receive her license? If Angelica received her driver's license based on the comfort of the car, should I require her to take the test again? Should she drive a less attractive vehicle next time? My thoughts continued to wander as I sat in the window of the vehicle registration office, the sun rising and beaming through the windows of the air-conditioned waiting room. The parking lot stretched like a desert in front of me. I continued to look toward the horizon of this vast, uninviting desert, willing my car to return with only a bump or two, preferably on the passenger's side.

Then a mirage appeared from the distance. A gold car glided across the parking lot like an Arabian knight galloping across desert land, triumphantly completing one battle and in search of a new quest. Angelica leapt from the car and bounced across the parking lot's warming tarmac, the examiner walking slightly ahead of her. Although Angelica was trying not to smile, an inward beam told the whole story she had passed. I wish I could have captured the next few minutes of adoration, affection, and delight that my daughter bestowed on me. It continued as we completed the relevant paperwork and took the final "mug shot" before her license was printed. A warm feeling of contentment oozed through my body. I was a mother who was appreciated, respected, and loved by my daughter. The months of persistence had paid off.

When safely seated and buckled in the car, I started asking Angelica many questions about her test. I was trying to discern whether the test had been complete and thorough. Angelica answered in as few words as possible. Then she hesitated, as if there was something bothering her. "Where's the emergency brake?" she asked, puzzled. "The examiner asked me where the emergency brake was. I told her we didn't have them on this model Jaguar."

This one statement has become the center of many jokes in our family over the years. My response is always the same, "I guess that's what happens when you let Mummy be the primary driving instructor!"

We were now classified in some anonymous database under "Family-of-five: three drivers, two cars." Presuming there is such a classification, it comes with a detailed schedule of assignments and activities. Cars are expertly juggled between drivers who have daily tasks and anticipated deadlines. The classification requires a level of professional juggling only seen in Cirque du Soleil. A world-class juggling team must practice hours together to ensure its performance is fine-tuned to the point of perfection. Competencies include teamwork, trust, and communication, which are mixed with a little humor and showmanship. Similarly, a family juggling two cars among three people must work for the good of the team, but Angelica never recognized that fact. She never appeared cognizant of the level of gas in the tank. Many times I would jump in my car, minutes behind schedule, only to find my full tank of gas from two days before was nearly empty. Juggling cars also takes trust, but many times when Angelica was supposed to pick up her brothers and drop them off at karate, she decided to leave them at their grandma's house in favor of another high school football game instead. Juggling cars takes communication, but Angelica would go out repeatedly, wandering aimlessly around in my car, forgetting to pick up packages I had requested. And juggling cars also takes a little wit. One day while I waited for my food at a drive-thru, a young lady at a cash register kept looking curiously in my direction. Finally she came to the window with a puzzled look on her face. "Your car looks just like my friend's car," she stated.

"Who's you friend?" I asked casually.

"Angelica," she said proudly.

"I am Angelica's mother. She let me borrow her three-year-new Jaguar."

With the puzzle solved, the young lady went back to her duties behind the counter.

On the trip home, I pondered my response and the young lady's reaction. Surely she didn't really think it was Angelica's car? I believe she did!

The incident at the drive-thru was one of the final motivations for adding another car to our family. The thought that our sixteen-year-old daughter was driving around the city in a Jaguar, claiming the car as her own, was not a value Aaron and I wanted to instill. We both come from working-class families where nothing was handed to us and hard work was expected and celebrated. Our one-family, two-car, three-driver classification was coming to an end; we were moving into a new phase: one family, three cars, three drivers, and even more headaches. Although Angelica secretly expected that we would purchase a car for her, she was happy when her father bought a secondhand Volvo for himself, and she received his 1996 Kia. Of course it wasn't a Jaguar, and it came with a smoky exhaust pipe, slightly fading paint, a broken door handle, and a very loud engine. But it was *her* Kia.

The Kia, my husband would explain, was the car that would help to shape Angelica's character. It would build her resilience, persistence, and desire for better. It would create hellish memories that Angelica would be able to (exaggeratedly) tell her grandchildren: "When I was your age, I had to walk miles through the sweltering hot sun of Florida's humid summers after my twenty-year-old car broke down on the way to school in the middle of an eighteen-lane expressway."

Within weeks of Angelica taking ownership of her car, the air-conditioning stopped working. This would not be a big deal in London, where summer temperatures peak in the seventies. In Florida, humidity determines whether a summer day will be pleasantly hot or unbearably scorching. Whereas winter heating is a requirement in England, air-conditioning in both houses and cars is classified as a necessity in Florida. Angelica's first challenge was to look cool in her car when she had no air-conditioning unit blowing 92-degree air on a humid, 110-degree day.

Angelica's second challenge was counting her blessings in all situations and circumstances because within weeks of the air breaking, one of the engine belts popped. Fortunately she was on the down slope of a very long bridge and was able to cruise, without an engine, to an emergency lane at the bottom. Her brothers were in the vehicle asking a series of whys. Angelica began the first of a number of emergency calls. But rather than dialing 911 as she'd done as a toddler, this time she called her father.

This episode signaled the beginning of a chronic series of belt problems. It felt as if we dropped Angelica's car off every other week to have a belt replaced. The beginning of the end of Angelica's character-building exercise started when she heard a knocking in her engine. She said the noise sounded like a little man was sitting in her engine with a hammer, rhythmically knocking on various parts. Angelica pulled the car over and parked precariously in the emergency lane of an expressway that took a sharp right curve, and then she called her father. The critically sick Kia was whisked off to a mechanic. The engine needed to be replaced. As with the other challenges, Angelica took this new problem in stride, not sure whether to take the events as orchestrated tests or just Murphy's Law of Averages. However, Aaron and I knew it was time to buy Angelica a more reliable car, one that didn't require her father's full-time attention and Angelica's full-time patience.

In her junior year of high school, Angelica started to plant seeds about the type of new car she would like, trying to influence Aaron's and my decision. Her stories were like commercial teasers being implanted subversively into our heads, popping out when we passed the right BMW car dealership. We received a running list of selective stories regarding the types of cars her friends' parents were purchasing for their sons and daughters. Maybe "The Jones Effect" argument would work with most parents, but it had the opposite effect on her father. Neither Aaron nor I had a point of reference for anyone purchasing us a car. Neither of us woke up one day at the age of sixteen and had a brand new car awaiting us in the driveway with a large red bow positioned expertly on top and keys with our names on them sitting in the ignition. However, Angelica's lack of reliable transportation was causing a certain degree of stress in our lives, and it was this force that made us decide to purchase her a new car. Aaron had already decided he would narrow the search down before inviting Angelica to make the final decision.

One warm Saturday morning, Aaron and I set off on a car-buying mission, but we soon realized we did not have the same idea of what mission success would look like. It soon became clear Aaron had a more geekish view of the car we should purchase, while I wanted the car to be fashionable and attractive to a teenage girl. Our discussions centered on whether a car could shape a person's personality or merely complement it. Aaron argued a geek car would propel Angelica into the class of elite students just by its sheer presence. I felt like a new car, the *right* new car, would stimulate Angelica into entering the class of high-performing college students. The car Aaron had initially targeted for purchase reflected the personality of a seventeen-year-old boy with a perfect SAT score and 4.0 grade-point average. However, after a few hours of subtle hints and questioning by his wife, Aaron decided we should call Angelica and let her make the decision. The wonders of early twenty-first century Internet enabled her to review the range of standard options and colors and quickly eliminate Aaron's chosen vehicle from our search. I secretly celebrated victory.

We drifted to various other dealerships before reaching our second planned destination. At this point I had caught the American dream of buying my daughter a brand spanking new car with a big red bow on top. Aaron remained practical, although he was at least slightly influenced by my festive spirit. Memories of our impromptu Christmas shopping sprees brightened my spirit further. I was not only delighted that Aaron and I were able to narrow our search down to two vehicles, but we were working together with a sense of single-mindedness as we sought to purchase a reasonably priced new car before sunset.

Marriages go through many times of being tested, but advanced testing of a marriage does not begin until children arrive. To be considered an expert in marriage, specific stressful tests must be accomplished with little or no squabbling. Aaron and I had been together looking at cars and discussing dealerships all day. We didn't always agree, and listening to car salesmen's idle chat and high-pressure salesmanship was not helping our increasingly tense moods. We had planned on being finished by three o'clock, leaving the remainder of the afternoon for leisurely activities we could enjoy together. It was now seven o'clock, the sun was going down, and we had not finished the purchase of the car, but we remained together, happy in each other's company and the lack of anticipated discord.

We were down to two cars at the last dealership. Again, the wonders of the Internet allowed us to patch Angelica into the discussion. The question was simple, especially for an eighteen-year-old eager to receive the key to her new car. Did Angelica like model A or B? If she didn't like either, the search would be put on hold for another day. For a teenage girl craving her freedom, another day seemed like another century. Waiting for an upcoming Saturday when all the stars would align in a manner that ensured her parents would shop for a car again was out of the question. Model A was the choice. Definitely model A.

Once the decision was made, I felt a combination of joy and trepidation. My mind drifted back to my childhood and the sacrifices my mother made just to put food on the table. A sense of guilt rose from my stomach at the thought of bestowing a gift of such luxury on my daughter. Then my rational brain started to remember my mother's dreams and promises for my children and me. My mother's greatest desire was a brighter future for her daughter and grandchildren. The salesman was completing the final paperwork when my mind snapped back to reality. He was asking whether we wanted a large red bow or balloons placed on the silver 2005 Saturn something-or-other model when Angelica picked it up early the next day. I instantly requested the bow and asked for the keys to be waiting for Angelica in the car. My mother's responsibility was to ensure I grew up to be a responsible member of British society despite the bad times. In turn, my responsibility was to ensure my daughter grew up to be a responsible member of our American society despite the good times.

Some people might say their most vivid memory of their child and their first car is the point they give their child the keys and the child jumps in and drives off for the first time on his or her own. My clearest memory involves Angelica, her new Saturn, and a police officer one Saturday evening. Angelica had been driving by herself for several months. That Saturday evening at about nine thirty, the house phone rang, and Aaron quickly answered, more concerned about not waking up the boys, who were fast asleep in their beds, rather than who was on the other line. It was a police officer. The officer said he had a policy that when he first pulled over a teenage driver, he gave him or her an option either to get a ticket with a steep fine attached or a warning. Of course, who wouldn't take the warning? But it came with the requirement that the officer talk to the teenager's parents so they were aware of their young adult's reckless driving. Angelica reluctantly chose the warning, knowing that she couldn't afford a ticket. After giving the reason for his call, the officer provided details on the reason he had stopped Angelica. Angelica had been driving ten miles over the speed limit in a thirty-five-mile-an-hour residential zone. However, speeding on the residential road was not the main issue. Angelica was also weaving in and out of traffic and not using her indicators. Her driving behavior was not only a danger to her but also to her passengers and to other drivers on the road. Once the officer finished, Aaron calmly thanked him for his act of caring and then patiently awaited Angelica's return. As he waited, Aaron wondered whether Angelica would choose to cut her evening merriment short, instinctively knowing that staying out later would make an already volatile situation worse. She did not.

Just before her curfew, Angelica arrived home, appearing apathetic toward her pending doom. Of course, I heard this whole story secondhand through my husband, and as with most men, the dramatic details were excluded. Angelica was cautioned by her father, just as she was by the policeman. Aaron and I both hoped and prayed that the lesson would become etched in her memory every time she got behind the wheel of a car. Many tickets and classes later, we realized it was not.

Chapter Five

"Angelica's college journey, like most of my dreams for her, had a different reality."

The Arrival of Almost Adulthood

My most coherent memories of Angelica as a teenager reaching toward adulthood revolve around finding the right next-step for her life. At times her journey was perilous. Oftentimes she preferred to discover her own path through riotous misfortunes, and frequently her journey took her through tumultuous trials. Yet she always remained determined and persistent.

Angelica's nineteenth year was full of firsts. One that stands out for me was her first traffic violation as an adult. Angelica was semi-gainfully employed at her college, working part-time in the recruitment office.

Aaron was very proud of his daughter. She had graduated from one of the top high schools in the county (Stanton College Preparatory High School) and was now in college. However, as the guardian of the family finances, he was eager to remove Angelica (at least partially) from the family payroll. Angelica, as a full-time college freshman, was responsible for paying for all her personal incidentals: clothes, hair, nails, entertainment, and, yes, traffic violation fines.

As I recount this tale, I can almost hear Aaron rejoicing when Angelica received her first ticket: "Oh, happy days, oh, happy days!" Aaron received a certain degree of consolation as he watched Angelica's sorrowful face. He knew the car was fine and she was fine. Conversely, her bank account might need several months of intensive-care treatment. The moment confirmed a natural, circular justice in the world. Angelica had received a failure-to-yield ticket. Aaron had spent the previous two years paying for homecoming dresses, senior pictures, graduation paraphernalia and regalia, and for countless other demands. The enormity of Angelica's senior year bills had not only stretched our bank account but Aaron's patience, too. Watching Angelica exhibit similar levels of frustration at a ticket provided a level of therapeutic reward. Aaron's appearance and mood lifted, and he was invigorated in a manner usually bestowed only by a six-week vacation in Hawaii on a private beach. Of course, to show his true maturity, Aaron's jubilation was only exhibited when Angelica was absent. Luckily her absences were quite frequent—she had a ticket to pay for!

Angelica remained rather secretive throughout the whole ordeal. It took several months after her receipt of the ticket for the whole story to unfold. During this period, she brought a definite attitude of righteous indignation peppered with a feeling of bewilderment to any conversation about "the event." "The event" became undiscussable in Angelica's presence, similar to the deepest, darkest, clandestine family event. The story began as a simple traffic citation for an illegal U-turn or similar violation. When the policeman stopped Angelica, she had neither her registration card nor updated insurance information. She received what we presumed was a large fine, but the ticket could be cut in half if she presented her registration card and updated insurance information within a certain number of days of the citation date. As the story began to morph, Angelica kept reminding us that she was sick the night of the incident. She repeatedly told us about the week she suffered in bed with the flu after receiving the ticket. Her righteous anger had rationalized that spending a week in bed was punishment enough. She felt it was unfair that the documentation, fine, and possibly a driver's education class should continue to be required. Her faulty reasoning demanded that these items should be dropped from her punishment. Her indignation dragged on, as did the deadline for documentation, fine payment, and possible class attendance. Angelica would say she procrastinated; I would say she waited almost patiently for her parents to come to the rescue like we had done previously. But we didn't come to her rescue. The time kept ticking, and the deadline kept looming. Within hours of reaching the deadline and the certainty of additional fines, Angelica completed her remaining obligations. It was only at this point that the whole story morphed into a comprehensive scenario.

Yes, Angelica had made an illegal U-turn, but as with other facts, she had withheld the location of the event, the campus of her college. With these additional details, Aaron and I both explained that her righteous indignation could have been appealed to a college board. In turn, the board might have accepted her personal petition and changed the penalty to a warning.

My emotions, as always, were mixed about this and similar instances while Angelica was in college. I understood: it was time for Angelica to take responsibility for her own mistakes. But I also understood my daughter's sense of righteous indignation. I wished I had channeled her emotions in a manner that enabled her to appeal the fine properly rather than having her sulk around the house every time the status of her ticket was mentioned above a whisper. I concluded that we were entering a new phase of our relationship, a stage where I could clearly remember walking in her shoes and experiencing the joys and the hurts of similar experiences. I had wanted to be both an autonomous adult and helpless child, oftentimes in the same minute. However, as much as I could remember the walk, it wasn't my walk. I could walk next to Angelica, encouraging her in her journey, in front of her, guiding her along rocky roads, or behind her, preventing her fall. However, I couldn't walk in her shoes. This was her journey, her frustrations, and her delights. And the tickets and the ticket-like stories continued, including her car almost being towed twice in a two-week period.

The story of the towed car started late one Saturday night when we heard a loud knock on the door. When Aaron went to answer, he found a local Jacksonville policeman standing on our doorstep. The Clay County police, a contiguous county, had called the Jacksonville police force about an abandoned car. After reviewing records, we were identified as the owners. As Aaron repeated the story, I could imagine the whimsical look on his face as he stared at our two cars parked safely in our driveway. The officer went on to ask whether Aaron had had a car stolen. Again Aaron looked past the officer to our vehicles, patiently waiting for the policeman to acknowledge their existence. As the officer started to describe the car, Aaron realized the officer was talking about Angelica's 2005 Saturn.

Aaron hadn't initially considered the Saturn because it had been impounded earlier that week, after Angelica had parked under a "DO NOT PARK TOW AWAY ZONE" sign. When Angelica was dropped off at home after her car was towed, she had insisted that the sign was not visible at night. She did not realize she was illegally parked until she left the "establishment" and couldn't find her car.

The next few days were agonizing for Aaron and me. We lived with an adult with no car but who had endless obligations. Aaron and I calculated it would take Angelica several weeks to save the money to pay her car's ransom. The question was whether we could survive the excruciating pain of living with Angelica until she had the money. Or were we willing to lend her the funds? After much consideration, Aaron and I decided when asked, we would lend Angelica the money. But she never asked. Then came the late Saturday knock on the door.

After the officer left, Aaron tried to decide what to do. He told me to call Angelica, and I did.

The rest of the story was pieced together after Aaron pulled his daughter home in the driver's seat of her Saturn very early the next Sunday morning.

Angelica decided that as soon as she had the money, she would go and get her car. She worked many extra waitress shifts that week, and by Saturday afternoon, she had enough to pay for her impounded car. After she got off work, she had a friend drive her to the impound lot located in the next county. She handed over all the money she had made that week and every last dollar from her bank account. The clerk handed over the key, and Angelica jumped into her car, planning to enjoy her newly regained freedom. By now it was early Saturday evening, and the sun was setting. Within minutes of leaving the facility where her car had been impounded, Angelica's car broke down right outside a high school and right in front of another "Do Not Park Tow Away Zone."

It was starting to get dark. After attempting to start her car a few times, Angelica pondered her next steps. Instead of calling her father, she called an old high school friend who lived nearby. After spending an hour or so trying to start Angelica's car, the friend gave up and planned on taking her home. That's when I was able to reach Angelica on the phone. She and her friend had driven a few miles from her car, but they agreed to quickly turn around and go back before the car got towed *again.* About an hour later, her father arrived to provide a begrudging, early-Sunday-morning tow home.

American College Life: A Naturalized Citizen's Nightmare

Unlike my husband's upbringing, I was always told I was going to college. My father had graduated from a British college, and my mother had all the brains but none of the right circumstances to attend. Angelica watched both Aaron and me struggle to complete five degrees between us (he has one more master's degree than I do) after we were married. Many of the important milestones in our marriage were eclipsed by college: My thirtieth birthday was spent in an evening, graduate-level tax research class. The birth of our last son included Aaron bringing books to the hospital to study for semester finals. We spent the first seventeen years of our marriage attending college in some form or another.

At an early age, Angelica learned college was important to us. In fact, there were times I wanted to quit school and spend the time with my baby girl. However, my husband's persuasive appeals always won over. "It's more important to Angelica that you finish college than spend the evening with her," he would repeatedly remind me during my emotional breakdowns. He was right. He also felt obligated. Many years earlier, as a strange consolation prize to my mother for losing her daughter "across the pond," Aaron had promised her I would finish college.

Angelica's college journey, like most of my dreams for her, had a different reality. We had initially planned for her to go away for college, but a combination of factors, including the end of long-committed relationship with her first boyfriend, made that impractical. However, college remained an important next-step for the three of us. Aaron and I were happy for Angelica to attend the state college we had attended. But we agreed, based on her request, to the local university.

Plan Number One: Since Angelica did not have a college scholarship, she would stay home for the first two years and attend the local university, the University of North Florida. In turn, Aaron and I would pay for her tuition, fees, books, and incidentals, such as her car, car insurance, health care, and general board. We considered letting Angelica live on campus, but since she was in the same town, it seemed reasonable that she stay at home and help save a little money. Her major would be pre-pharmacy. This choice of major was very surprising because I had not heard Angelica discuss pharmacy before and didn't know she had an interest. Aaron reminded me that her uncle, Aaron's older brother, had casually mentioned it several times. Aaron presumed his brother's wise words had rubbed off. Oh.

Angelica's first year went reasonably well. Her college-prep high school classes made the freshman year of college a breeze. Furthermore, her first love was hundreds of miles away at school in Tallahassee. We had agreed that after two years she could transfer to the college of her choice in Florida.

Little did we know that by the beginning of her second year, Angelica was ready for her freedom. Unlike her ancestors who had to wait for the Emancipation Proclamation, she just needed her own source of income. Unbeknownst to us, she had picked up a waitress position while also keeping her part-time job on campus. By this time we had developed a tradition of sitting down around the dining room table when it came to discussing serious family matters such as grades, sex, and oh, did I mention school grades? Angelica requested a meeting. She wanted to let us know that she had been waiting tables for a couple of months and had saved enough money to move closer to campus. We were in shock, but after much discussion and debate, Plan Number Two was executed.

Plan Number Two: Angelica would move closer to campus and share an apartment with three friends. Aaron and I would continue to pay for her tuition, fees, books, and incidentals. However, she needed to maintain As and Bs in all of her classes. Angelica would pay for her apartment, which was shared with three other girls.

Aaron and I were not happy about the compromise because we wanted Angelica to focus on school rather than be burdened with monthly rent and various other life demands. However, Angelica had made up her mind—she was determined to move out. We were resolute that she would finish college, so it seemed this was the less-than-happy concession we had to make.

Her move was very sad for me. I felt as if I had let her down but couldn't quiet determine what I had done wrong. As she packed her room, I kept peeking in to watch her progress. At one point, I slipped in to give her a massive hug. In return there was nothing. I knew Angelica clearly felt hurt, and I sensed she wanted me to understand her position. I felt I did understand and had lived her viewpoint with many life scars to prove it. I wanted Angelica to understand rather than live my lifetime of faults.

In preparation for her move the next day, Angelica left several loads of large black garbage bags next to the door, each filled with her life's belongings. When I came home from work that night, they were gone. All that was left of her possessions was a small garbage bag of memories. Hanging in her bedroom closet were the three dresses I had bought her for her first part-time job. There was also a collection of stuffed toys. As I picked up and admired each of the toys, a series of comforting memories popped into my head. Each memory marked so many wonderful times, uninterrupted by the pains of the present. I sat crossed legged on the floor of Angelica's room and determined to confront these memories as I rummaged through the garbage bag. There were so many photos, including photos from Angelica's senior year dance and prom. Photographs Angelica had demanded we purchase, as if her life depended on their existence. Now they were just tossed away as meaningless pieces of paper. I systematically went through the garbage bag and removed all the precious memories. I knew she would want them one day.

After Angelica moved out, we did not see her for long periods of time. Generally her appearances or calls coincided with her beginning-of-semester requests for tuition funds. In fact, I only visited her apartment once, a few months before her lease was up and she planned on moving home. I was impressed with its neatness, but it didn't feel like home. Looking back on the experience, I am not sure what we could have done differently, but the year cost us *big* time.

Angelica requested another one of our family meetings. It had been awhile, and as usual, she was full of surprises and excuses. She had been working too hard and taking too many classes in an attempt to finish quickly. She was stressed, frazzled, and drained. She wanted to come home. Of course, we opened our arms and door widely, but even the move back cost us money—seven hundred dollars of additional fees and Angelica's deposit because she had decided to paint her room red (among other things). But she was home.

Plan Number Three (similar to Plan Number One): Angelica would stay home. We would continue to pay for her tuition, fees, books, and incidentals. We also discussed grade requirements, but Aaron and I didn't enact them. We were just glad she was home.

The move to an apartment had been *our* fault in Angelica's mind: we had been too restrictive. In turn, Aaron and I relented on our demands. Angelica agreed to…well, she did change her major again—pre-dentistry. Did we know that? "Not exactly" was the only response I could get from my emotionally drained, stoic, marine husband. Oh.

Angelica completed her junior year with few hitches. At about the end of her junior year, she declared she had never wanted to be a pre-pharmacist-medical-dental major: we made her do it! Well, I guess that was a relief. She had always wanted to be a psychologist and had been working toward this major the last two semesters. This degree required at least a master's degree in mental health counseling and probably a doctorate degree, too. At this point there was silence. Aaron and I looked mutually stunned. Angelica requested a meeting. We demurred. She had clearly determined her own next steps.

Plan Number Four: Angelica moved out. She said it would be better this time. We paid no tuition, no fees, no books, and her car was paid for. We didn't mention car insurance, and we didn't mention health or dental care. After the first semester, we did reimburse her for her As, maybe Bs, and possibly Cs.

* * *

The moment of Angelica's graduation was a dream I had played out in my head many times as Angelica "found" herself at college. It generally would include her walking triumphantly on stage and receiving her diploma with a little smile on her face. The actual week of Angelica's graduation was full of many family activities: we were moving, I was going out of town on business, and Aaron IV was getting his braces off. It felt as if the significance of Angelica's graduation was being concealed by the many activities and events of our busy family.

Angelica declared that she wasn't going to attend her graduation; I had mixed emotions. She had worked so hard, persisted, and grown into a truly impressive young lady. I felt it was reason to celebrate. However, I also understood her hesitation and desire just to move on. It was time.

We decided to create a memory-filled family dinner at her restaurant of choice: an Italian restaurant, Buca Di Peppo. I knew the moment was going to be special when Aaron's mother, who rarely left the house, decided to join us. The exact details of the event are blurred. It resembled how an out-of-body experience might feel. My baby girl was sitting there with her best friend, laughing, grinning, and picking at her food. I wanted to capture the moment in a snow globe, sit the globe in a prominent place next to my bed, then replay the event with the shake of my hand, or just stare into the memory as it replayed in my mind. From the outside looking in, there was nothing spectacular about the event. It was simply a family gathering for dinner. But to me it celebrated the end of a chapter in life, a slice of time to pause and be thankful for the journey accomplished and the lessons learned. It was a mother and her baby girl celebrating the end of a turbulent passage in their always-connected lives.

Printed in Great Britain
by Amazon.co.uk, Ltd.,
Marston Gate.